Mastering the Deal

M&A INSIGHTS FOR THE 21ST CENTURY LEADER

Nitin Kumar

Authors: Nitin Kumar

DISCLAIMER

The contents of this book are not professional advice to guarantee success; the book is for educational purposes only. These observations, takeaways, and observations are based on our experiences with Management Consulting and Executive Roles.

Contents

LEGAL NOTES

The publisher and the author are providing this book and its contents on an "as is" basis and make no representations or warranties of any kind about this book or its contents. In addition, the publisher and the author assume no responsibility for errors, inaccuracies, omissions, or any other inconsistencies herein. The content of this book is for informational purposes only and is not intended to diagnose, treat, cure, or prevent the commercial, operational, or financial position of a company or individual. This book is not intended as a substitute for the admission process of each Firm.

Using this book implies your acceptance of this disclaimer. The publisher and the author make no guarantees about the level of success you may experience by following the advice and strategies in this book, and you accept the risk that results will differ for everyone. The testimonials and examples provided in this book show exceptional results, which may not apply to the average reader, and are not intended to represent or guarantee you will achieve the same or similar results as the individuals or companies mentioned.

Dedicated to all the unsung warriors in M&A who have created so much value for their shareholders

Preface

After spending several years in the M&A world globally, I published a few thoughts, experiences, insights are learnings over the years.

I have led hundreds of due diligences spanning across Commercial, Operational, Technical, and Customer bodies of work. Led over 75 integrations and 25 divestiture separations, ranging from the small to the mega-deals. Having spent so many years in M&A, making many mistakes, observing behaviors, and delivering success. I have shared my thoughts on various forums like LinkedIn, Medium, Podcasts, and a variety of forums.

There was never any intent to write a book amalgamating the disjointed bodies of knowledge and thoughts, until some clients I served, my M&A network, friends, and people who have followed by blogs, soundbites, and other forms of social media urged me to do so.

Why? What did they think that I could do differently from being yet another book on the shelf?

These professionals felt that my articles often provided useful frameworks for understanding niche issues in the due diligence and M&A integration process where well-defined literature around those topics was not available. They thought these experiences could enhance their M&A thinking and deal execution.

There have been several books written on M&A, some of which have been best sellers and helped to teach me the basics of integration in my early days too. The problem is that business has changed a lot over the last decade, but M&A has largely remained the same without adapting much, there are areas beyond the basics and these new scenarios but have no formal literature around them.

Many of my clients and M&A network has been frustrated with the lack of guidance in the "new" approaches to M&A or expansion of existing bodies of knowledge.

Encouraged by these comments and reactions from C-level executives, M&A integration leaders, business unit leaders, and other accomplished executives hungry for more topics, I spoke with them on what they would like to see under the so-called "lesser-known topics". During this process, I spoke to scores of executives, polled several through surveys, and used social media to gather the areas in which these advanced topics were more sought.

In polling these executives, I was fascinated by the response that some issues were common between large companies, mid-market, and private equity firms, and hence wove some of my higher impact content together in this form.

The unified voice tacitly said that they all knew what the good ingredients of a "traditional" M&A were and largely knew the basics. Some even though they might have a one-off gap in specific functional areas, for which they could get help externally. Some executives stated that they viewed the acquisition engine of their respective organizations as a core capability viewed to be a competitive advantage. They were all grappling with the problem of how to take this capability to the next level and enhance their competitive advantage.

The results out coincided with my own belief there were several advanced topics out there requiring attention, however not everything was a common scenario. I used my experience and judgment to focus on a few topics that would make sense to consolidate. I have published several articles on these topics before ranging from Turnaround of broken M&A efforts, Integrating Hostile Takeovers, and Managing Information Risk during M&A's which met with overwhelming responses as these advanced and niche topics were never written about before.

I will not be going into the basics of post-merger integration and mention how to go about its part by part but will be headed straight for frameworks, models, strategies, and tactics ranging from due diligence to M&A integration of various functions. The structure of the book is very modular, and I have tried my best to make sure that you could read each chapter independently of each other depending on which areas interest you. I do hope this book gives you insight into several topics you could put into practice either immediately or as M&A goes through a paradigm shift.

Who should read this book?

Executives running businesses where they have identified M&A as the growth strategy. This book will be valuable to consultants who practice M&A due diligence, integration, corporate development professionals, and anyone who would like to take their basic knowledge of M&A to the next level. I hope that executives, professionals, and other readers can use the book, its data, its diagnostics, and its principles to make more informed decisions around M&A efforts.

It is assumed some of these topics, frameworks, and tools will get embedded into the core capability of an organization they grow through M&A. In addition, investors and private equity firms should find the frameworks and literature useful in evaluating their portfolios and asking the right questions.

My promise to readers

Today there are dozens of tools and analytical techniques applied to the M&A world, especially in M&A.

My promise is that I will not add to the existing clutter of literature or offer hope through this book. What I offer is a collection of small bite-sized nuggets of wisdom to shape your thinking, these are built on real-life experiences and tested in multiple deal scenarios. The content of this book reveals several niche areas in the M&A and are problems that surface from time and again, they could help businesses increase their odds of success during the execution of deals.

The book is also meant for due diligence and post-merger integration pros who could catapult their knowledge to the next level by gearing themselves for the topics which will continue to surface at a greater frequency as M&A becomes more complex.

This book is not written in the spirit of being a business book, a detailed DIY manual, or being too strategic or too tactical. You will find a little everything here given how it came together. The main objective of this book is to get you thinking about these lesser-known areas and facets of M&A, not meant to be a comprehensive guide.

Next generation M&A

As the business world gets more complicated in the coming years, several of today's advanced topics will become commonplace and the need to keep up and master these and emerging areas of the discipline will become a necessity towards value creation through M&A.

Happy Reading and Happy Thinking!

"In the 21st century business landscape, M&A is no longer just about numbers on a balance sheet. It's about the strategic mastery of integration, where leaders navigate complexities with the precision of a well-executed wargame." – Nitin Kumar, "Mastering the Deal: M&A Insights for the 21st Century Leader"

1

Creating Value from e-commerce M&A Integration

Over the past few years, we have seen the 'pure click' retail industry i.e., a 100% digital business model with no physical presence, some familiar businesses are GILT, Flowers.com, etc. Traditional brick and mortar companies are now transitioning to 'brick and click' business models and sometimes walking away from the traditional brick model.

The retail industry's growth hinges upon its ability to exploit the digital trend, given the loss of foot traffic in traditional stores with a further decline expected. Given this shift, companies are looking to acquire new business models which can bolster their sales through new digital channels.

Key revenue drivers include:

- Acquiring, retaining, and servicing customers through PCs, mobile phones, tablets, video game consoles, smart TVs, AR/VR, and voice-operated assistants, etc.
- Increased ability to track, predict shopping patterns online, and target specific advertising campaigns. Metrics like MAU (monthly active users), DAU (daily active users), etc. have become mainstream and trackable.
- Increased sophistication of e-commerce platforms providing top-notch user experiences.
- Competitive shopping opportunity for users and data-driven sales for sellers.

E-commerce companies are also looking to exploit new trends such as personalization, advertising, re-targeting, new distribution channels, marketing, and customer experience design to drive customer engagement and revenue enhancement. Companies have figured out innovative ways to sell products digitally and sell products digital native products.

Key trends include:

- Ability to sell globally
- Infinite shelf space
- Social media selling
- Peer-to-peer selling
- Social gaming
- Search engine-based selling

Most companies today have e-commerce or will soon embark on it. M&A transactions in the e-commerce space are driven by consolidations mergers, some distressed M&A, and large volumes of companies trying to acquire or migrate to a new business model.

Most of the value is created in the M&A integration phase; to create value, one needs to understand the core value drivers within an e-commerce transaction. Based on my own experience, I have listed a few below (non-exhaustive list).

e-commerce M&A: Core Value-Creating Actions

- Understand similarities in existing e-commerce business models 80/20 rules vs higher product concentration e.g. (95/5 rule) versus more diluted product sales.
- Document similarities and differences in customer segments within e-commerce and isolate high-performing and high-potential customer segments.
- Target may sell digital media or other products or services that embody intellectual property (how does this compare with the buyer) - are there subscription models at play?
- Develop customer retention strategies and safety nets for Day One (focus high

performing and high-potential customer segments).

- Create a cross-functional team across sales, marketing, service, pricing to develop mitigation plans across possible Day One issues such as brand protection, customer retention, and service disruption, talent defection, etc.
- Core e-commerce value drivers need to be identified, the typical value lies in (1) Active users (2) Active Customers (3) Talent (4) Technology Platform - understand what needs to be protected (Day One) and what needs to be enhanced (Beyond Day One) across both organizations.
- Understand and document data flows across both e-commerce platforms, including interfaces with other front-office and back-office systems.
- Ensure policy level alignment across buyer and target; typical policies include website accessibility, privacy,

terms of use, social media, safety, and
security.

- Harmonize and integrate other
compliance considerations for Day One
- compliance with the law, binding
website users across jurisdictions,
appropriate disclaimers, and
limitations of liability; understand when
customer contracts are used (B2B)
instead of standard terms.
- How do suppliers' contracts across
both companies impact the target
operating model (across both
companies) - confidentiality, availability,
liability, credit card, and payment
controls, etc.?
- Target's brand (trademarks and
domain name) may be a key
component of Target's value, how does
brand transition occur (if applicable)?
- Target may have developed proprietary
software or other technology that

creates an important competitive advantage (how can this be preserved?)

- Target may have patents or trade secrets relating to business methods, algorithms, processes, or other technologies (how can these be monetized?)
- Content of target's website, including its 'look and feel', may be protected by copyrights and contributes to rich customer experience (understand similarities and differences with the buyer).
- Website hosting - Possible source of synergy; considerations based on in-house capability, service levels required for the target operating model, and third-party ecosystem reliability across both companies.

Every value driver does not apply to every transaction, both priority and applicability can vary depending on the transaction.

The ability to conduct business through channels like web, mobile, VR, and voice are driving M&A volumes steadily. The ability to understand value drivers and create value through M&A integration is just beginning.

2

M&A Due Diligence, Evaluating Artificial Intelligence Deals

The M&A market has been hot regarding acquiring AI companies. Most companies now view AI as essential, existential, and table stakes. The two main drivers of these deals have been:

(1) Address gaps or enhance capabilities of their existing technology stacks

(2) Race to acquire AI talent for the future i.e., acqui-hire transaction

The valuations have been high and driven by strategic rationale, the immediacy of needs, speed to market, timing, and seller expectations.

AI companies come in a variety of flavors e.g., some of the legacy big data folks now rebranding themselves as AI with highly optimized rules, but far from being cognitive in their capabilities. These companies are also in various stages of the life cycle e.g., one having just the vision and talent, some have IP, others have a viable product, few have paid customers and a very limited universe of standalone AI start-ups have operating profit and scale. IP valuations can get contentious with proprietary technology and algorithms having no standard value measurements with patents enhancing value.

Founders and CEOs of AI companies know that they must focus their pitch on strategic valuation rather than traditional valuation drivers like sales, EBITDA, or even ARR multiples today. Most traditional acquirers and investors and wired for operational metrics-based valuation with AI or other disruptive technologies, this is breaking down today. The discounting methods do not hold today as AI companies are not willing to take a zero premium as many know their potential ability to accelerate the growth trajectory of acquirers, reduce costs, enhance customer experience, differentiate in the market, simply survive, or add vital capabilities for the future.

Talent valuation of acqui-hire transactions plays out differently on the value spectrum i.e., based on the technical credentials and track record of the personnel, level of cohesion, or tenure/history of working together. The industry thumb rule puts acqui-hires values are between $1 and 1.5m per employee, but AI companies go as high as $2.5m per employee (Source: Magister group research). Strategic acquirers must understand the market, the premiums and evaluate those against their strategic fit. The valuation rationale must also justify the IRR of an AI acqui-hire > 3x of organic hiring.

Buyers must answer several key questions when looking at an AI asset.

Key questions and considerations (non-exhaustive list) to seek during AI due diligence and valuation would be:

- Is this truly AI or big data/other technologies layers with an AI wrapper (plenty of those out there)?
- Where is the value concentrated e.g., algorithm, specific part of the tech stack, background of people, team cohesion, vision of founders, etc.?
- Does the AI company bring in direct revenue enhancing speed to market, unlock additional insights, create a new market, augment existing products,

and what does the revenue acceleration projection look like?

- Can the AI deliver at scale? For example, are there limitations based on the data source, volume, structure, etc.?
- Does the AI company create cost efficiencies, productivity gains, and meaningful automation, and what part of those can add to the buyer EBITDA and what % can be passed onto the customers? What do those projections look like?
- How much boost does the existing analytics capability get? What is its timing and when does one feel the impact?
- How scalable is the technology, what is the threshold of impact where it breaks down?
- What is the performance and how does it get affected by scale or change of environment?

- Is the technology stable, does all functionality work the way it is supposed to?
- What is the source and sustainability of competitive advantage? How replicable it is by others in the market?
- Does it have a risk of obsolescence?
- How extensible and interoperable is it?
- What are security features and how secure are they?
- Is there non-standard technology used, what is the impact on maintainability?
- Is the knowledge documented and well understood or is it tribal with few developers and architects?
- What are R&D processes, approval cycles, and investments in future features?
- Are there compliance risks?
- How much open source is used and what risks do they bring to the company?

- How does the acquired product, feature, or technology create synergy through integration?
- What is the strength of the management team, can they execute the next big vision and strategy?

AI will be embedded into everything we do; it will just be the new normal and a way of everyday life. The possibilities with AI are just limitless as it can open many new capabilities and new markets. The M&A race for AI has just begun and there will be a lot of M&A activity in the days to come.

3

M&A Integration: Services Function

In the digital age, we are transitioning into business models where traditional products are being delivered as services. Mainstream trends such as cloud, IoT, etc. have altered consumption mechanisms, the evolution of social and mobile have created new channels for customers to interact and consume services in real-time. 80% of the customers use at least 3 channels expecting immediate and cohesive experience across them all. Service functions always touch the customer and is a critical ingredient of customer experience and business continuity.

Service is more than just customer support, it covers "as a service" business model, elements of customer experience, and even professional services.

In the M&A integration realm, services are moving from being a value driver of cost synergy towards creating revenue synergies. In several business models, services are already a profit center hence paying specific attention to M&A integration realities would ensure protection and creation of transaction value.

During my experience in integrating service functions, I have come across multiple value drivers - to realize the value, multiple questions need to be answered. I have provided a non-exhaustive list below:

- What are the differences in service models (level of automation, self-

service vs individual touch, method of
service consumption, etc.)?

- What are key operational similarities in
the way services are provided between
the two organizations i.e., service
quality, service levels, delivery
mechanisms, KPIs, etc.?

- Where are revenue synergies being
created e.g., combining products and
services, expanding portfolio of
services, or enhancing customer
experience/ service quality or
complementary/supplementary service
s, etc.?

- Are there services, delivery processes,
or technologies that can be rationalized
in the combined entity?

- What are key differences in SLAs,
pricing, and contracts?

- What are key customer touchpoints?
What interaction models exist at those
touchpoints? What aspects of the

touchpoints need to be preserved and
which ones need to be enhanced?

- Are there opportunities to migrate to
service-based business models e.g.,
software licenses to SaaS
or infrastructure to IaaS and platforms
to PaaS, etc.?

- Are services configured as cost centers?
Are there opportunities to migrate to
profit centers or vice versa?

- If professional services are involved,
what are the similarities and
differences in leverage, rate, margin,
and utilization of resources?

- If call centers of customer support are
involved then understand channel
capacity i.e., mobile, chat, email, phone,
etc. Can a combined company maintain
optimal capacity and channel harmony,
or will imbalances be created affecting
staffing levels?

Do not forget the usual synergies from headcount, process, contracts, and asset rationalization.

Given many industries are in transition to "as a service business model", the service function becomes a key driver of value in the near-term M&A landscape. Hence the integration of the service function to protect, capture and create value will be important.

4

M&A Integration of Loyalty Programs

The core purpose of a loyalty program is to instill repeat buying behavior from customers through incentivizing them to stay and measure buying patterns; loyalty programs are becoming important for B2B too, although its roots lie in traditional B2C businesses. During an M&A integration, loyalty programs can be leveraged to drive cost and revenue synergies while retaining customers in a time of flux and change within the organization.

Some specific areas where loyalty programs are useful to protect, capture and create value would be:

- Increased customer intelligence

- Ability to design engagement,
- Promotion strategies,
- Profitability shifts,
- Customer retention and acquisition when cross-selling teams are ready.

Success with loyalty programs requires a strategic and thoughtful approach with a multi-lens plan during M&A integration.

Loyalty Strategy

Understand the similarities and differences between the two companies with a commitment to customers across similar dimensions i.e., one company might want to enhance the experience through discounts/redemption in their products while others might open it up to several partners to foster a better and wider experience. The integrated programs must be cohesive and not conflict with each other. Objectives range from acquiring new customers, making existing customers more profitable, use consumer loyalty attributes and behaviors delivering relevant/personalized experiences, and improving up-sell, cross-sell, and wallet share. It also makes sense to compare the CLTV of the two companies attributed to the loyalty programs themselves.

Omnichannel Considerations

Omnichannel engagement represents the largest risks and opportunities. Permitting loyal customers to connect and navigate to accounts or enabling products to deliver consistent information such as loyalty points, promotions, or redemption processing, etc. Delivering this experience across multiple channels such as website, chat, e-commerce, contact center, mobile, social networks, email, direct mail, newsletters, member statements, events, voice, and POS is a lot of work.

Watch out for channel equilibrium imbalances e.g., the volume designed for chat inflows or mobiles might far exceed (or be under-served) because of integrating two companies with disparate channel usage and planned capacities. Ensure proper routing, queue optimization, and incentive-based channel migration where applicable.

Program Positioning

Understand relative positioning, strengths, and perception of each loyalty program across both companies. Align the loyalty program with the brand message, brand promise, and vision of the combined entity.

Differentiating to attract and retain customers is important; surveys have revealed that customers value three attributes in a loyalty program i.e., simplicity, trust, and transparency. Focusing on these attributes upfront and building them into the integration execution needs capital creating tension with synergy objectives and longer-term value. Based on my experience, I have seen customer retention and acquisition costs get lower over time to offset the investment upfront, and synergies (or lack of) pays for themselves in the longer term.

Measures

Tracking, monitoring, and reporting loyalty program status, its KPIs, and customer incentives are a leading practice to drive incremental transaction value. Customer segments are distinct (even within the same company) and hence homogeneous application of policy, process, or cost spreads could get counterproductive and leak value from the transaction.

Incentives must be relevant and valuable enough for consumers to join and remain in the loyalty program. They should be allocated using a tiered approach to encourage higher spending levels with more significant rewards. Key KPIs such as retention, new sign-ups, cost of acquisition, cost of retention, cross-sell benefits, up-sell statistics, CLTV, reward rates, break rates, etc. should be reported regularly through the IMO.

Deploy pattern identification as practice with contact centers to proactively address defection patters and additional buying patterns.

Day One Planning and Execution
Critical Success Factors for day one is centered on protecting customer touchpoints, ensuring relevance (campaigns, promotions, etc.) are not diluted with no negative customer experiences, service quality and service levels must adhere to brand promise ensuring early trust and credibility.

Alignment between CX, Loyalty, Marketing Operations, and all customer-facing functions must be in place and appear cohesive to end customers. Think of day one as laying the foundation for delivering revenue synergies as the integration progresses.

Technology Integration
The technology systems must integrate well to ensure smooth integration of loyalty programs, multiple critical systems such as CDP, CRM, ERP, Point of Sale, BI systems, and GIS (Geographical Information Systems) must be woven together to ensure data integration and information flow to and from the L2C (Lead to Cash) process.

Synergies
Understand the impact on cross-selling and upsell value drivers, impact on areas such as customer experience. Isolate impact by customer segment and analyze value drivers distinctly. The one size fits all strategy rarely works, companies should focus on aspects of loyalty that can

enhance product (or feature) adoption and create incremental revenue synergies.

Loyalty Marketing Automation

It is commonly observed that companies (to optimize cost) will think of the loyalty system replacing marketing campaigns, loyalty systems cannot typically deliver on this. Instead, seamless integration of loyalty with marketing systems activates customer activity, online behavior, and buying history from both companies and creates personas and ideal customer profiles.

This can help enhance relevance, create new personas, make targeting (and retargeting) more relevant to accelerate revenue synergy realization.

Customer Segmentation

Customer segmentation is the foundational element to integrating loyalty programs, the combined customer segmentation should be done early in the deal process. Activating a cleanroom is a leading practice to ensure velocity and momentum.

It enables sending more personalized/relevant content to targeted groups generating higher engagement, conversions, and yields. Think beyond demographics and purchase histories and include attributes such as interests, lifestyles, usage patterns, trends, events, and life stages, etc. It can also help identify customer segments delivering the highest profits to the companies and those absorbing profits. In addition, uplift modeling can be applied through gaining a unified view of consumer intelligence acquired from loyalty program tracking (and other systems from both companies) with predictive analytics to maximize margin and retention.

Typical impact to customers occurs due to changes in policy, systems, and operations creating positive, neutral, or negative experiences. Safety nets to retain customers, catalysts to extract new customers and get delivering better experiences to existing customers and enticing them to pay more can stem from the design and execution of loyalty programs.

Loyalty program members generate 12%-18% incremental revenue per year, compared to non-members. Loyalty program members generate 12%-18% incremental revenue per year, compared to non-members.

Loyalty Program Integration Risks

There are several risks with loyalty programs even in the way they are implemented before the transaction, and M&A integration-like scenario could break these aspects.

Watch out, scrap, de-risk, or transition programs or adjust the design if you see these patterns:

- A program valid only to attract customers through a first transaction e.g., sign-up, and I will give x thousand points, this will get costly to use during an integration given systems are not geared to attract new customer segments and the one-time stuff rarely works, a byproduct is an added cost eating into synergies.
- A 100% system reliance with no human touchpoints can alienate key customers, possible system glitches due to integration will compound the problem. Make sure there are safety nets and manual business continuity in place before executing automated loyalty and CX integration.
- Zero engagement - if you notice no sign-up process and no meaningful

customer data capture it usually means no engagement and likely no returns. Over time it if one company does it better than the other, it will create data imbalances, skew surveys, and customer schemas. Use M&A integration as a catalyst to drive higher ROI through investment, engagement and migrate away from the free, easy, and zero value game.

- Understanding ICP (Ideal Customer Profiles) and managing personas are important for creating customer loyalty. This is specifically important when customer data is being integrated, if not done properly you could show baby toys to octogenarians etc. Understand how loyalty value is created, distributed, and exchanged across every customer segment in both companies. Map personas and manage outliers without compromising synergies.

As M&A drives new consumption-oriented business models such as SaaS, SDN, IoT, AI, Big Data, AI, and OTT or enabled by these technologies. There will be more competition for customer stickiness, engagement and to monetize those business models. Paradigm shifts will occur in customer loyalty programs and how you focus on integrating loyalty programs.

Companies have been Taking loyalty M&A integration seriously in more recent times, assigning their own workstream.

5

Leveraging Disruptive Tech in M&A

In today's increasingly digital world, conventional business models are being disrupted and new paradigms are being created. In certain cases, like M&A transaction execution (both integration and separation), multiple opportunities avail themselves to accelerate value creation by adopting an "asset lean" approach.

IT (Information Technology) is one of the most complex functions with traditional integration or separation, arguably creating the most synergies, the highest operational risk and adding most of the cost. Server virtualization (think VMWare), cloud, and lately SD-WAN provide a lot of opportunities to drive synergies faster with far lesser execution risk. Centralized orchestration and policy-based management allow for minimizing design, configuration, and implementation of features/functionality at a device or node level reducing the need for extensive manual labor, errors, and rework.

Let us discuss this at a more tactical level.

Software-Defined Networking/ SD-WAN

During an event like a Merger, Acquisition, or Divestiture - several cycles of design are required at the network level of technology infrastructure with activities spanning cabling, data center migration, network architecture, traffic engineering, IP addressing and network security, etc. risking misconfiguration, delays and/or unplanned outages.

SD-WAN avoids a lot of this work. SD-WAN can also prioritize traffic and conserve bandwidth based on applications by routing lower priority traffic through alternate paths.

It is a common practice during integration or separation to virtualize servers and migrate applications to the cloud where applicable creating more flexibility, SD-WAN can provide similar benefits to the network layer. Multiple advantages range from reduced implementation costs, faster execution, minimized day one risks, enhanced time to synergy realization, and speed to market help maximize transaction value.

While this migration might not be an intuitive investment for one-off or occasional acquirers, frequent and serial acquirers will benefit tremendously by adopting SD-WAN quickly.

Artificial Intelligence

AI is not a single technology stack but a convergence of various technologies, statistical models, learning algorithms, pattern recognition, and approaches to drive business benefits. This taken to the next level creates Cognitive Computing involving self-learning using data mining and pattern recognition and simulate the way human brains would approach problems. In the M&A integration context, any business application enabled by AI with the ability to reason through data, establish relationships connecting data sets is a superior due diligence asset for acquisitive companies.

These cognitive systems can be applied to areas such as customer insights, revenue synergy targeting, contact reviews, supply chain optimization, etc. for better accuracy and deeper inspection of possible deal issues. Other areas where AI can be deployed are closing financial books, customer experience, stability of service levels, and service quality in shared services environments, etc.

Drones

Supply chains have become complex entities today and one can optimize them for speed, risk, cost, etc. Deploying AI (as mentioned above) can itself bear fruit looking at reconfiguring the network to align and harness deal value quickly. Drones and deploying them can help create a lot of value when the two companies have distributed assets, inventory that needs to be mobilized, and speed of delivery creates customer value.

Drones can help map the network quickly during diligence, work with AI to optimize synergies, and lastly solve the last mile problems persistent with the merging of two complex supply chains. When coupled with AI, it can yield favorable deal value through levers like contract renegotiation, supplier, and customer optimization, etc.

The disruptive technologies are already gaining mainstream adoption and will be real in the next 0-12 months disrupting the way we look at M&A Integration and Separation.

There are several more technologies e.g., RPA, Cloud, 3-D printing, and VR with their niche applications that will reconfigure the execution of M&A. It is a matter of time when these technologies scale and go mainstream.

6

Cybersecurity in M&A

Digital, the most overused and abused word in the industry today, making organizations scramble to consolidate their positions in this new world. Many are taking the non-organic route [i.e., mergers and acquisitions (M&A)] to acquire digital capabilities and assets.

The transition to the digital economy also brings cyber security to the forefront when evaluating these target companies and the security posture of their digital assets. Today, ransomware and the weaponization of sensitive data are real threats as malicious actors use sophisticated techniques to attack organizations, heightening the need for cyber security due diligence.

Traditional due-diligence exercises have focused on the quality of earnings, operational assessments, legal risks, and IT in some form (with cyber being a small bullet-point covered under the IT body of work). With cyber-security issues capable of disrupting the flow of operations, reputations, cannibalizing assets etc., executives should realize the potential risks to their brand, customer confidence, insurance premiums, valuation, incident remediation costs, and eventually investor confidence. These factors are contributing to the rise of cyber-security due diligence as a standalone body of work when assessing the suitability of a target company to acquire.

Understanding Cyber Due Diligence

Assessing the posture of a target company's security requires thinking beyond traditional checklist assessments used to evaluate compliance and canned, tool-based security scans. The short due-diligence timeframes, low cyber security acumen of management and issues with quality and completeness of company data create additional challenges during the cyber security M&A due diligence of a target company.

There are three flavors of cyber-security due diligence and acquirers can decide the level of assessment they undertake toward evaluating risks.

Red Flags Review

The quick and dirty version of a cyber-security due diligence typically includes requesting high-priority information and reports from the target company and validating then through analysis, management interviews, and corroborating it with the team's prior assessment of similar target companies. The next step is to quickly document "red flag" issues and initiate further drill-down on those specific areas in a surgical manner during the confirmatory due diligence phase.

Test Reviews

This level of review typically encompasses the detailed assessment of multiple areas of cyber security and can include running intrusive scans if the information submitted by the target does not meet expectations. Characteristic areas of technical assessment include data-center security, network security, storage controls, end-user posture, applications, third-party risks, data controls, etc. It is also a good practice to interview key personnel and understand the level of security awareness in the organization. More specific details are provided in the sections below.

Landscape Review

The highest level of review usually entails a detailed scan of the target company's entire threat landscape for existing, new, and emerging threats and documenting the risk level associated with each vector. One way to do this would be to assess the landscape and understand whether malicious groups could access the infrastructure, applications, or data of the target. Also included in this step would be to evaluate the attack vectors, points of vulnerability, mechanisms and speed of response, cost of controls/response teams, or risks due to the lack thereof.

Landscape assessments should also factor in the change of location due to integration of the two companies.

Typical areas of M&A Cyber-security Due Diligence

Cyber-Security Strategy

Understand and document the overall cyber-security strategy and its alignment levels with the overall business strategy, IT strategy, and the company's product portfolio. Typical gaps arise when the cyber-security strategy is skewed too much into IT or gets very compliance centric. A good cyber security strategy should align with the business and core operations of the company. Make sure the gaps due to the strategic direction are captured well.

Governance

Document the governance structure and processes of the company (e.g., who is involved in direction setting, defining priorities, ensuring level of alignment, deciding, level of rigor, reporting, etc.). Assess the impact of the governance of

the organization on the cyber-risk posture
of the company.

Organization
Evaluate the cyber-security organization,
including structure, size, skill sets, and
staffing by functional area. Assess the
leadership and the culture of the cyber-
security organization to assess the fit.
Identify and analyze the value/impact of
existing third parties in use to provide
cost-effective or specialized services.
Document the risks due to skills, staffing
levels and structure, etc. Understand the
level of security awareness and acumen in
the organization and assess human
weaknesses in the overall security posture.

Infrastructure
Evaluate the risk associated with the core
IT infrastructure components, including
datacenter, network (WAN/LAN), desktops,
hardware, and office automation tools
(e.g., messaging, file, and print, etc.).

Identify potential business risks and/or improvement opportunities.

Applications

Evaluate the security and privacy posture of major business systems providing automation and support to the core operating processes. Understand the financial impact associated with the confidentiality, availability, agility, and integrity of each. Assess the ability to log, monitor, track, and report timely and accurate cyber security-related metrics and information.

Data

Understand key data flows through the organization, ensure no PII data-related risks are assumed, and that controls are in place. Review data creation, data acquisition, data modification, data transmission, data storage, and data disposal; make certain they are well understood. At each phase of the data cycle, the controls should reflect the value and risk of data regarding the organization and the threat landscape.

Operations

Review all policies and procedures in place. Assess whether they are aligned with the cyber strategy, the compliance needs of the organization, and there is a consistency of awareness regarding policies and procedures such as authentication, access control, business continuity, passwords, incident response, etc. Document the ability to enforce, manage, monitor, track, and report across multiple areas, locations, and controls. Document any possible risks and gaps.

Prior History

Review prior incident history including breaches, outages, audit reports, etc. Understand root causes, response procedures, mitigation plans, and continuous improvement. Review all existing and prior vulnerability assessments, IT audits, and penetration testing reports to ascertain the rigor and discipline of testing to document all risks and opportunities.

Spend and Budget
Analyze overall cyber-security expenditure plans and budgets (both capital and operating expenses) regarding strategic objectives and risk profiles. Understand historical spending levels regarding industry trends, benchmarks, and best practices.

Key Initiatives/Projects
Identify and profile significant, capital-intensive cyber-security projects as plans or in process. Evaluate the status, strategic value (regarding management's objectives), feasibility of cost and timelines, and potential business/execution risks.

Integration Planning

Assess the overall cyber-security integration strategy, identifying synergy opportunities associated with consolidating environments, infrastructure, redundant controls, locations, vendors, contracts, licenses, and organizations. Understand the key integration projects and initiatives, including the one-time costs, timing, and level of effort. Understand factors such as the new regulation compliance, probability of success, resource constraints, and conflicting projects that could affect cost/timing of synergy realization or assume new risks attributed to the changed threat landscape.

Always analyze the full stack i.e., datacenter, network, storage, end user computing and applications etc. document risks across each layer and impact on other layers. The target company is only as vulnerable as its weakest link. The _Yahoo_ and _Equifax_ like scenarios will only grow unless acquirers give adequate importance to cyber security due diligence.

"The modern M&A leader doesn't just close deals; they orchestrate a symphony of cultures, technologies, and talents. 'Mastering the Deal' unveils the secrets behind successful M&A in today's fast-paced world, where integration is the true measure of leadership."

7

M&A Integration and Acqui-hires

Acqui-hires has entered the vocabulary of M&A professionals recently. Many stories of organizations translate the art of such deals into science of succeeding with it, but there are also horror stories about such transactions. Although, 'digital' business models have taken the acqui-hire concept even outside of technology companies, the bulk of these deals are still entrenched in the TMT (Tech, Media, and Telecom - in that order) sectors.

Companies who master the art of acqui-hiring can enhance speed to market for their products by adding niche technical and operational talent. These skills fill critical product development needs or increase depth of certain markets and sectors. Although multiple acqui-hire deals appear remarkably similar in concept, there are similarities and differences.

Similarities

- Driven by shortfall of engineering talent or highly skilled and specialized workers.
- Talent typically comes from start-ups to accelerate hiring e.g., NPV of acqui-hire > organic recruitment execution.
- Cohesive teams working together. Typically, founders have prior working experience with Product Dev executives of the acquirer.
- In country, offshore resources are unlikely acqui-hire candidates (many are now making exceptions)

Differences

- Transactions can be originated by corporate development or even engineering leaders. Speed from identification to deal close, transaction

- evaluation metrics and motives can vary based on origination.
- Accompanying business or products can be kept alive or wound down based on level of compatibility with acquirers' strategy.
- Level of cohesion, maturity, price, and motive could vary based on whether they are in the Series A vs Series B stage
- Angels' vs venture capitalists funding can create multiple third-party stakeholders with different motives.

Acqui-hire transactions are not all the same. Investors rarely are entitled proportional shares of the value of the company e.g., a $5 million acqui-hire could cause the investor getting some insignificant fraction even if they own 35% of the company. Given that all employees are being hired and original operations will go away, the target must pay off debts where applicable and equity ownership does not matter as much. It will be a better deal for investors to get something rather than a shut down and write-off if the asset is not growing as planned or is stressed, but this has triggered a sleuth of emotions and debate in the Silicon Valley circles.

The higher the number of investors, the more complexities there will be in getting an acqui-hire transaction done. Investors do and can trigger blocking rights in the terms of their funding agreements if they wanted to.

Having advised many clients on a few of these transactions, here are observations and lessons learned:

Product vs Sales Culture

It is generally a well-known fact that most Silicon Valley founders and CEOs have a strong bent towards either sales or product/engineering, they build cultures based on this affinity and hire people aligned with that mindset. Even though the average worker bee appears to be made from the same technical fabric, it is a much harder transition from a sales-oriented culture to a product oriented one and vice versa. A like-to-like transition has a much higher probability of success.

Talent Retention = Transaction Value

Typically, acqui-hires are not the dollar windfall that people would have hoped for leaving some of the acquired employees yearning for that. Some equity (or options where applicable) will create the motivation for these hires to stay engaged, incentivized to create value in the organization, and not get distracted by the next shiny start-up promising wealth creation. In my experience, cash retention bonuses seldom work, and that cash is a tool triggers the clock to exit.

Set expectations with fair value of equity, options, and future grants based on results and value created by incoming team. Acqui-hires are typically pegged at ~$1 million per employee, slightly higher if there is there is IP, patents, longer tenures, early customer traction etc. Industry practices suggest acquired employees get a salary, some stock with approx. 4-year vesting period and a much smaller cash bonus. Certain acqui-hire transaction terms require all (or the majority) of the hired group to stay at the acquirer for 3-4 years, employee turnover below a certain threshold will cause the whole team to lose money.

Manage Executive Repatriation

One needs to pay specific attention to the skills and background of acquired executives. It is getting increasingly common to see people to grow into leadership positions e.g., Vice Presidents in large traditional organizations and then transition into smaller start-ups with similar titles. While larger organizations tend to 'title down' people from start-ups by calibrating them against the size, span, and job complexity of the acquirer - specific attention must be given to the personnel who had marched up the executive ranks in prior jobs based on their caliber and experience in similar organizations. "Under titling" and under fitting them could lay a platform for discontentment and ultimately departure.

Bigger is Better

As ironic as it might sound, acqui-hires success rate has been higher in bigger organizations acquiring smaller. The bigger the difference, the better the chances of success. A smaller differential creates a false sense of 'merger of equals' creating conflicts on strategy, products, policies, priorities, and management styles. Specifically, conflicts are highest in the sales vs product issues, decision making and investments.

Brand Matters

An acqui-hire transaction is never driven by the urge to re-brand a company, hence the brand transition needs to be quick to ensure a sense of identity and belonging through messaging in a positive manner. A unified brand, be it local, regional, or global, creates clarity, consistency, loyalty and reinforces the purpose of the transaction. Not changing or delaying brand transition, can prolong the 'us vs them' mindset.

Manage Change (Both Sides)

The mindset of the acquired organization needs to be managed carefully. Existing employees have worked hard, stayed loyal and created a company capable of acquiring. The acqui-hires sharing the same floor and cafeteria now have earned much more money for just on-boarding through an acqui-hire transaction. There are no easy answers to cracking the code on this one - at least not yet. On more than one occasion, I have been vented to by employees of acquiring companies. Even though most may not quit instantly, it gets them thinking if it was a ticket to easy and quick money.

Employee Experience is Critical

Managing employee experience is an important lever when integrating acqui-hires. The three big buckets that can make such experiences positive, neutral, or negative are centered in policies, operations, and systems (culture encompasses these), also not all employees are equally affected by each area. Assess employee engagement and segment them based in what the acquirer learns. Designing safety nets and risk mitigation strategies need to be informed by data and analysis. A simple framework on how to think about this is given below (% indicates % of employees). Typical examples of safety nets are training, communication, autonomy, incentives, mentors/sponsors, affiliations, and even well-organized change management programs.

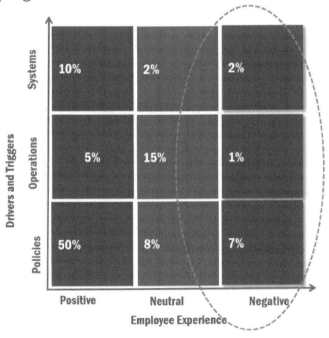

Figure 1: Indicative Employee Experience Impact Grid

Measure Success

Multiple Silicon Valley companies have deployed the acqui-hire strategy, be it Google, Facebook, Microsoft, or Yahoo, some have even done multiple deals with higher success rates. The key question is how to measure success and what metrics to deploy to track the ROI from such acquisitions.

Here are a few examples I have worked with (non-exhaustive list):

- Time to close the transaction.
- 'Productivity day one' (on-boarding effectiveness)
- % Employees retained after 12 months
- % Executives retained after 12 months
- Acqui-hire NPV of current transaction > NPV of prior transaction > NPV of organic recruitment
- Employee engagement scores
- Skill transfer rate (to acquirer)

Although there have been mixed feelings across the board regarding Acqui-hires in the investor, founder, acquirer and acqui-hires themselves, this trend is likely to continue with some years having more transactions than others. Acqui-hire transactions can be smoothened by using simple guiding principles with some mechanics still evolving.

8

M&A Decision Making

M&A Integration is an extraordinarily complex activity attributed to multiple functions, personnel, products, geographies, customers, unique nuances, dependencies, risks, and the sheer volume of tasks to be executed. Bringing all this together requires several decisions to be made in quick order. Decision making is part art and part science, seasoned M&A integration professionals understand the four Vs surrounding good decision making i.e., volume, velocity, value, and variety. How, when and where these integration related decisions are made can affect the end state of the integration and value creation from the transaction.

In a recent survey I conducted, approximately 100 M&A integration leaders were interviewed, here are insights from it:

- 61% believed slow speed or lack of decisions created sub-optimal value from the deal.
- 43% shared concerns about the quality of decision-making.
- 34% believed slower speed of decision-making affected synergies.
- 22% understood the differences between executive decisions in steady state operations and differences in an M&A integration environment.

The below figure can help throw some perspective on the volume and velocity of decisions during various business situations and how an M&A integration stands out.

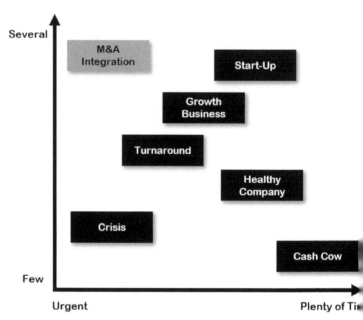

Figure 2: Decisions Framework

Understanding Variety of Decisions

Quality of decisions are causally related to its enablers, during a M&A integration we generally see many decisions with one or more enablers. Integration managers and leaders should quickly wrap their arms around each decision, its key enablers, the owners, and the impact of the decision itself. Making sure the right enablers are used will enhance the quality of decisions e.g., a decision requiring specific experts should not be made with data analysis or experience alone.

Figure 3: Decision Enablers

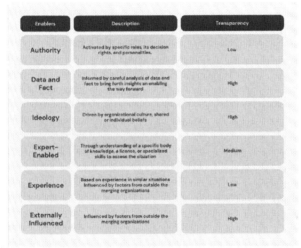

Each type of decision or its enabler has an inherent level of transparency attached to it - understanding the right enablers to each decision helps communicate the rationale ensuring higher levels of transparency. Quality of decisions can also be affected by style of decision making e.g., consensus vs unilateral etc., these are more cultural and should be undertaken based on what works in each organization. Understanding value of decisions is equally important e.g., At $100 million planned synergies, each week of delay due to lack of decisions postpones realization of ~$2 million in EBITDA.

Managing Decisions: Leading Practices

- Make sure everyone on the team understands the financial, operational, commercial, and legal aspects attributed to each decision or lack of it.
- Establish good governance to enable decision rights at the right levels in the organization early in the deal cycle e.g., at the due diligence stage itself.
- IMOs should facilitate the right decisions, by the right people using the right enablers.

- The more dissimilar the cultures the greater the need for definitive and timely integration decisions
- Decisions, at the right places will enable combined problem solving, set directions and rule out further discussions - decide upfront, especially the tougher ones.
- Establish the authority of each decision maker with clear lines of formality, interaction model and demarcation with other decision makers.
- Make sure culture and ideology-based decisions are communicated widely with proper understanding of the impact on integration.
- Enable and staff the integration with qualified personnel with the right and relevant skills – expertise-based decisions are required in specific areas such as legal, IT etc.
- Understand impact of external forces on decisions e.g., HSR, pressure

campaigns, regulations etc. and make sure impact is well understood.

- The IMO should include list open decisions in all status reports and seek timely closure from the right people.

9

R&D Integration in M&A

As the M&A landscape shifts from consolidation deals looking to deliver cost synergies from back-office functions to more revenue synergies from go-to-market, the role of R&D as a function and a source of synergies becomes more important. It is one function that enables both cost and revenue synergies from a deal.

The sectors I typically operate in i.e., TMT (Tech, Media, and Telecom), access to new capabilities, R&D, and technical talent are often cited as the top three M&A drivers. R&D can be one of the highest value creation functions if the integration is handled well, often R&D is set aside. Typically, insufficient resources are invested upfront in the due diligence creating integration challenges downstream.

Synergies in most functions can be realized within weeks (cost take out) or months (revenue growth), R&D in certain situations takes years to produce tangible but lasting value in terms of synergy. Executing a sound M&A integration plan can shorten the value creation cycle by several months or even years. Measuring values from R&D and tracking them over a period is critical, value drivers are centered on four areas:

- Shorter development cycles
- Higher R&D productivity
- Increased speed to market
- Lower cost of development

M&A Integration should also be viewed as a catalyst to reduce complexities in the combined portfolio of the merged entities.

A few key considerations to maximize value from the R&D portfolio would be:

- Opportunities for cost synergies:
    - Too many products or features serving the same purpose.
    - Multiple platforms with inefficient leverage
    - Unneeded and unmonetizable functionality and features
    - NPI/EOL complexities i.e., new products co-existing with old ones for too long
    - Insufficient leverage of designs and modules across products
    - Rationalizing organization, facilities, systems, platforms, and tools
    - Unifying processes to create efficiencies.

- Opportunities for revenue synergies:
    - Aligning clock speed of both R&D organizations with market demand

- Redefining pricing mechanism in line with product profitability
- NPI (New Product Introdution) and/or new feature introduction through unified roadmaps
- Aligning product fitment to reflect brand positioning.
- Retaining key R&D talent
- Fitment of products and speed to market with existing channel structure
- Harmonized R&D pipeline, product, and technology strategy

In my experience working with several R&D organizations, there are four distinct strategies one can pursue towards R&D Integration:

Strategies	Attributes	Perspective	Pros	Cons
Market Centric	• Leading or following market trends • Competitive advantage building • Proactive/preemptive or responsive/resolve • Preserve culture of target (if applicable)	Typically, either minimal or partial integration to preserve and maintain competitive advantage trading off any immediate synergies	R&D that worked well previously need not be disrupted but cost synergies tend to be minimal, sound execution can enable some revenue synergies	R&D decisions often tend to have pre-acquisition biases and could send mixed messages to people Market responses or preemptive acquisitions need upfront investment possibly conflicting with cost reduction goals of traditional integration
Performance Centric	• Historical performance • Product shifts and trends • Feature and functionality oriented • Enhance output, reduce cost and increase speed to market	Historical data is used as a baseline to determine future state of integration	Analytics and data driven approach often focused on a single growth strategy i.e., within a single product or market. Reduces complexity and creates cost synergies	Historical baselines tend to be counterproductive towards transformation efforts
Customer Centric	• Breadth and depth of relationship • Customer loyalty, product experience and customized features/functionality • Needs, opportunity and customer demand driven	Objective of introducing new products and features to serve new or unmet needs within specific customers or segments	Works well in industries with higher customer concentration i.e., semiconductors	High degrees of customization are expensive and un-scalable where customer concentration is less
Portfolio Centric	• Product synergies, enhances stock adjacent products, capabilities or features • GTM synergies, leveraging reach or scale • Portfolio and market expansion	Portfolio of products need to be tightly aligned with market, customers, channels. R&D posture needs to be integrated or adjusted to support the combined portfolio	Tighter and full integration strategy can lay a platform to enable market and revenue synergies; cost synergies can be a favorable byproduct of tighter integrations	Understand cultural similarities and differences and develop mitigation plans to avoid conflicts and flight of talent

Figure 4:Strategies for R&D Integration

R&D Integration cannot be sidelined given the importance of products, speed to market, and disruptive trends in the marketplace today, even though realizing R&D integration is more complex, higher risk, and longer time to realization than other functions. In today's fast-paced and disruptive world there could be nothing worse than weakening your innovation capabilities through poor R&D integration.

Keeping R&D departments separate, being too cautious of culture and execution risk diminishes immediate synergy and elongate time to value than partially or integrating them.

Executives need to pay specific attention to R&D given its high impact on businesses and entire product ecosystems. This function cannot be sitting on the sidelines anymore, there is just too much at stake.

10

Blockchain Due Diligence

Blockchain technology can change how consumers share and store data through secured chains of cryptographic blocks. Not only can blockchain revolutionize currency, but it can also codify areas such as events, medical records, transaction processing, voting and so much more. Over the last few years, I have evaluated many Blockchain technologies from an M&A and valuation standpoint, also having been in the Blockchain and crypto ecosystem for many years and acquiring a few credentials in this space, I have developed my own framework on how to evaluate some the intrinsic value within Blockchain technologies.

An Overview of Blockchain Technology

The formation of blockchain technology comprises linked blocks, each of which holds numerical information often found in databases. These blocks link together and build off the previous one to form a chain of data blocks (aka, the blockchain). Blockchain technology is an open-source ledger, meaning that all participants are privy to the same information. The ledger method of validation eliminates the double-spending problem, which arises when an individual sends the same money to multiple sources.

The technology is thus run on a p2p network where there is a set protocol for creating and validating transactions in new blocks. Popular applications of blockchain such as Bitcoin operate on an open ledger, while some uses of blockchain, such as government initiatives and voting, may benefit from a closed-source chain or a partially closed ledger.

The advantages of blockchain include the decentralization of user data, which is achieved through the public network of participants who form a consensus that the information presented is accurate. Instead of one entity or corporation having control of the data, blockchain data is shared throughout its participants, where these users have the power to add code to a blockchain. Blockchain also creates the potential for crypto assets, which could move commodities into a tokenized set of crypto data to be used on a commercial level.

 Last, the popularity of blockchain technology gives way for new business models and propositions for companies that want to promote decentralized technology-oriented business models.

Evaluating Blockchain Technology

I will now explain a framework for evaluating Blockchain technologies and business models through three tests i.e., decentralization test, crypto-asset test, and a business model test.

Decentralization Test

Decentralization is the biggest driving force behind the shift to blockchain technology and business models. By decentralizing data on a public record, block-level data is transparent to all users. Since blockchain is decentralized, the coding is open source, so one entity does not own or control the information and decentralization grows stronger with the entrance of new users. The more people who engage in the network, the harder it is for an individual to censor information to the public. Blockchain technology is typically decentralized across one of four vectors: political, architectural, commercial, or contractual.

Let us take a deeper look:

Political Decentralization
Political decentralization refers to how many individuals or organizations control the system. Political decentralization strengthens as more people engage in blockchain activities — the more individuals, the less power each has over a single point of influence.

Architectural Decentralization
Architectural decentralization refers to the computational hardware and software required by a system to operate. Blockchain follows architectural decentralization because there is no central infrastructural point (i.e., no one computer at the center of the network). Many misguided companies repackage distributed computing as blockchain and

try to create a viable product or use case with a limited understanding of true technical decentralization. Be cautious of these.

Commercial Decentralization

Commercial decentralization refers to the business models and opportunities that a decentralized network creates. For example, a decentralized method of currency transaction disrupts the typical banking model with set fees and interest rates, enabling direct people-to-people transfer. It is a distributed business model moving away from aggregators and platforms shifting economics from aggregation to peer-to-peer with decentralized monetization models.

Contractual Decentralization: Contractual decentralization, known as "smart contracts," in blockchain technology, relies on the blockchain code to initiate a transaction between individuals. The contract is devoid of human mediation and initiates a transaction over well-orchestrated code and both parties have abided by the rules of the contract.

Crypto Asset Test

Crypto assets are another lens to evaluate the technology, it determines the behavior of the technology and its monetization potential. A crypto asset can take three forms i.e., a crypto commodity, a token, or a crypto currency.

Crypto Commodities

In the physical world, commodities are metals, oil, etc. creating finished goods, in the digital world they correspond to network, storage, compute, protocol, etc. helping create tokenized digital products. There are many crypto commodities like Ethereum, Cardano, etc. Within crypto commodities, more than one technology will likely scale based on use cases.

Tokens

Tokens are analogous to finished digital products built through crypto commodities. Although there are many solid use cases of tokens, a lot need not exist or have weak use cases. One needs to carefully consider how the crypto commodities build these tokens and whether the use cases create value. Some tokens are more valuable than others, while a few just ride the hype.

Crypto Currency

In my mind, there is only one true crypto currency which is bitcoin. There are several commodities and tokens implemented in a manner that can function as crypto currencies. The ability to monetize these implementations into either commodities or currencies can drive value, all else is far from reality.

Business Model Test

The final and critical test on whether the business model makes sense or how value is created, and a sustainable economic logic is visible. In the Blockchain world, ATOMIC (assets, trusts, ownership, money, identity, and contracts) are all programmable. The business model is created based on which one is these are monetized, what is subsidized and how dollars flow through the business. Understand how each of the above ties into a cohesive business model.

Based on my experiences, 90% of the entities fail the decentralization test, and of what is left 90% fail the crypto asset test. Of the products that make it through both above, approximately 50% either fail the business model test or need substantial tuning to create value and sustain their business. Blockchain is coming of age, but many misguided efforts

will need to filter out and ensure
identification of true value.

"Gone is the era of M&A as transaction; welcome to the epoch where M&A is transformation. M&A leaders, akin to alchemists, transmute challenges into value and visions into victories."

11

The Carve-in Transaction

Most people have heard of conventional M&A integration and Divestitures (be it carve-outs or spin-offs). However, the rare cases of carve-in transactions exist, albeit less prevalent than the former deal types. It does have its triggers, rationale, transaction process, nuances, and approach to integration which marginally differ from conventional M&A integration. Having had the good fortune of executing two of these during my career (both public companies), I thought I would share my thoughts on this topic.

What is a Carve-in?
A carve-in transaction refers to those deals when a parent wants to integrate or re-integrate a fully or partly owned subsidiary

into itself driven by various triggers such as market pressures, a mega-transaction resulting to threaten the existence of the subsidiary due to conflicts resulting from the transactions, drastic changes in the channel structure or business model changes due to acquisition of a new technology which promises to extract higher value from the integrated operations than a standalone subsidiary.

Although several nuances of conventional M&A integration are still relevant, the focus with carve-in integrations is on a variety of issues.

Here is a non-exhaustive list of some interesting differences:

Multiple Day Ones

Depending on whether the subsidiary is publicly traded or private, there are multiple Day One scenario

- De-listing Day One: This is when the entity is taken off the stock market and privatized, a very elaborate procedure and steps need to be followed to accomplish this.
- Legal Day One: When they are still operationally separate, but all assets, personnel, and contracts are operating under the parent legal entity structure.
- Operating Day One: Like integration Day One, the day when operational combination commences.

LEI (Legal Entity Integration)

Underlying complexities of legal entities need to be integrated/simplified; each LE owns its headcount, assets, costs, contracts, liabilities, and the absence of such a simplification can create operating challenges; careful analysis needs to be performed on optimizing legal entities for tax vs operating efficiencies vs triggering regulatory alarms. This can be a non-trivial process if there are multiple countries, currencies, and regulatory items to comply with

Change Control Mechanisms

If not carefully handled, carve-ins can trigger change control counter measures such as golden parachutes, poison pills, and the likes. These aspects will need to be assessed upfront during the due diligence.

Dis-synergies

While integrations are thought of as synergy creating, carve-ins have the potential to create dis-synergies if not handled appropriately. Re-integration can line up an array of channel conflicts insulated in the prior operating structure (specifically if it was not an owned subsidiary), similarly, there are other areas such as brand, products, and specific customer contracts which can spin up dis-synergies.

Synergies

Cost reduction or even revenue synergies are typically not the primary drivers of these transactions, the focus is typically on Beta synergies i.e., those synergies directly affecting the stock price of the new company. The synergy exercise is much focused on isolating, analyzing, executing, and communicating these Beta synergies to the capital markets.

As I mentioned, this is a non-exhaustive list in the spirit of highlighting differences. While I cannot reveal the specifics on the transactions I worked on, a hypothetical scenario would have been EMC carving in VMWare or HP carving in Mphasis - both those scenarios have now taken different turns but still work as a good possible example.

12

Technology Diligence, the Heart of Digital M&A

The business velocity, the exponential growth of technology, and the impact on business models create several opportunities for businesses.

Technology is transforming several industries enabled by digital: cloud computing, software-defined everything, internet of things, artificial intelligence, blockchain, and payment, etc. Every company wants to be a software company today, this is driving higher than ever M&A activity to catch up or gain a competitive advantage.

A few years ago, only technology companies acquired other technology companies but now, a lot of non-traditional competition has emerged for good technology assets, there are examples of media, retail, energy, healthcare, etc. all competing for technology stacks as they aspire to be digital businesses.

Companies today want to pivot their products, processes, or even business models towards digital – they bought assets enabling the acceleration of this transition as opposed to organically mobilize their transformation. The fierce competition for these technology target companies has driven up demand and valuation. Given the high prices, buyers now want to know the risks and opportunities associated with the technology creating a compelling need to conduct tech diligence.

I have seen technology diligence being confused with IT due diligence many times as people get caught up in the jargon confusing all technology to be the same.

- IT due diligence is usually conducted in the realm of the CIO i.e., back-office assets, enabling technologies, and processes. It is the part of technology within the SG&A.
- Technology due diligence is conducted on the product or a significant enabler of the product, usually, with the CTO, Business Units, digital units, etc., this is the part of technology that resides in the COGS. From an M&A standpoint, the focus is on understanding and evaluating the core engineering or technical competitive advantage underpinning the asset.

Both IT and Tech DD require different approaches, skill sets, resources, and experiences, technology diligences are more complex and require deeper, higher-end skill sets rooted in deep engineering with the ability to ascertain the source of value.

Tech DD tries to understand risks and opportunities towards the acquiring company's business case; inform the valuation process (what the acquirer will or should pay for the company or assets).

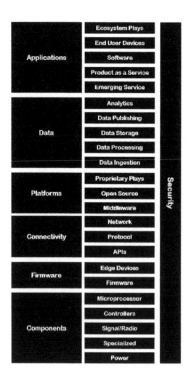

Figure 5: Typical Technology Stack

A typical stack has layers of technology weaved together to create functionality, uniqueness, and value. One needs to understand the risks and opportunities associated with each layer of the stack and a whole.

An example of the technology stack is provided in figure 5. Analyze each layer of the stack and the entire stack holistically to understand the risks and opportunities associated with the technology and its impact on existing and new business models.

It is also critical to understand the one-time costs and level of multi-year investments required to keep the technology running and evolve it toward commercial, operational, and technical trends of the future.

Good technology due to diligence professionals can also see through the layers of technology. I have run into wrappers of technology often when I have conducted these diligences. For example, I run across SaaS wrappers put above half-baked technologies that do not scale or support true multi-tenancy like a SaaS business. Hence it is traditional software packaged with a SaaS wrapper and does not merit a buyer paying SaaS valuation.

Machine learning is yet another area where wrappers are common today, several stacks do not have true cognitive ability or scale. This is a common target company posture given the demand for tech and talent in this space.

Key Question for Technology Due Diligence (non-exhaustive list)

- How scalable is the technology, what is the threshold of impact where it breaks down?

- What is the performance and how does it get affected by scale or change of environment?
- Is the technology stable, does all functionality work the way it is supposed to?
- Which specific part of the stack is the value locked in e.g., middleware, UI, algorithms, etc.?
- What is the source and sustainability of competitive advantage? How replicable it is by others in the market?
- Does it have a risk of obsolescence?
- How extensible and interoperable is it?
- Is it representing its valuation i.e., if the target says it is a SaaS product, is it a real SaaS with multi-tenancy, etc.?
- What are security features and how secure are they?
- Is there non-standard technology used, what is the impact on maintainability?

- Is the knowledge documented and well understood or is it tribal with few developers and architects?
- What are R&D processes, approval cycles, and investments in future features?
- Are there compliance risks?
- How much open source is used and what risks do they bring to the company?

13

M&A Integration: Using Complexity Reduction as a Value Driver

Most CEOs (start-ups through Fortune 500) or other C-level executives have told me they feel the nature and impact of complexity on their business. Their jobs are more stressful than a decade ago. This so-called complexity is only going on the rise with globalization, multiple regulations, disruptive business models, new competitors, changing customer preferences, more M&A, and a plethora of emerging technologies, etc.

The larger issue at play is most executives feeling the impact of complexity, but unable to dimension it well enough to resolve it. The solution to this lies in answering a few different questions:

- How does this complexity come into being?
- What causes it?
- How to dimension it or measure it?
- What levers could one pull to contain or eliminate it?
- How do we reduce enterprise complexity? Is M&A the answer?

Understanding Complexity

Foremost, complexity has a different size, shape, dimension, and form depending on where in the organization it is visualized from. For executives, complexity arises from the size of an organization, the diversity of the products, the several distribution channels, multi-country operations, cross the border, legal and tax issues, diversity of skills and competencies, disruptive competitors, and emerging technologies, etc.

For middle managers who often operate within a country, business or department worry less about executive definitions of complexity. For them, the complexity revolves around the ability to get their jobs done, the levels of authority, accountability, the clarity of their role, systems, and the business processes that enable their productivity, etc.

These different definitions of organization complexity versus individual complexity from different vantage points make one group oblivious to the other's issues. There are more people affected by the complexity at individual levels which cascade up or down and amplify existing company-level complexity.

Addressing Complexity

Another fundamental issue is that some of the complexity problems have been looked at in silos not organizationally. For example, executing an organization design initiative to minimize role overlaps, clear reporting relationships, and trying to resolve these issues often neglect nuances with specific functions e.g., IT, access control, etc., and transfer complexity from one area to another without eliminating it from the organization. organization-level complexity will not go away unless it is addressed holistically.

Measure Complexity

Measure complexity at the business process level at a minimum and not at a functional level. Metrics and benchmarks regarding complexity can be captured by looking at the variability of processes, average decision-making time, productivity, throughput of a business process, response, and resolution times to support or number of systems, level of automation, number of customer touchpoints, etc.

Good and Bad Complexity

Not all complexity is bad hence differentiating between good complexity versus bad complexity is important. Good complexity adds a competitive advantage due to its sophistication or makes it hard for the competition to replicate. Good complexity is always controlled whereas bad complexity is uncontrolled and drives ambiguity, reduces accountability, creates confusion, and takes a toll on productivity, and increases costs, it often grows at an alarming due to lack of proper controls or governance.

Let us understand this with an example, the planes of the 1950s and 60s which were accident-prone and crashed much more frequently on technical failures but today's planes although are a lot more complex and sophisticated but safer and more reliable, hence not all complexity is bad.

An organization likely has a mix of both good and bad complexity; therefore, understand the complexity profile of the enterprise before we mitigate it ensuring good complexity is preserved and the bad is eliminated.

M&A as a Driver

A transaction is a perfect catalyst to address and remove complexity from the combined organization. There are several value creation opportunities when we remove complexity from an organization including enhance speed to market, increased service levels, optimized costs, efficient systems, an effective organization, reduced variability, etc. Transactions not solely focused on cost but want to create operational competitive advantage should consider complexity reduction as a primary driver. Various phases of a transaction should address the reduction of complexity in different ways.

Due Diligence

Understand the geographic footprint, product mix, # of channels, organization structure, process/system variability, level of standardization, service levels, speed to market, etc. of each organization and document the required level of variability. Clearly define what needs to be protected i.e., good complexity, and what needs to eliminate i.e., bad complexity. The latter should inform the synergies and execution roadmap during integration planning. Cost synergy though is not the primary driver it is still a favorable byproduct. Document and dimension the revenue impact realized through speed to market and enhanced customer experience etc.

Integration Planning

The integration planning must factor in a variability reduction plan starting from the customer, markets, and products with the supporting processes, systems, and functions quickly enabling the plan. The right complexity reduction KPIs (both operational and commercial need to be set in place). All areas of risk should be documented, the big two risks typically are, the risk of transferring complexity from one function to another and not having developed mechanisms for permanently eliminating complexity at governance, process, personnel, and system level.

In my experience, complexity in any organization can fall into are four major profiles per the figure. Any organization with low levels of good and bad complexity is an unsophisticated business, while if the levels of good and bad complexity are high then the competitive advantage is negated due to the deadlock positions assumed between the two.

Before embarking on a complexity reduction, understand where your organization lies on this grid and try to reduce complexity holistically, also make sure processes are put in place to stop the reappearance of bad complexity.

Integration Execution

As with any other M&A value creation, execution is key. Ensure the IMO is not configured in a typical functional posture, but complexity drivers need to be tackled x-functionally and a value driver lead by complexity area is a good practice to follow. Complexity reduction is typically done in waves of twos or threes, with the first two taking 100 days or less (depending on the transaction) and wave 3 going longer. Typical scenario, wave 1 is an organization, products, channels, brands, etc., and wave 2 is processes, systems, facilities, and revisiting the organization structure, wave 3 is an area such as contracts, sales, reducing components from R&D/Products/Platforms, etc.

Reporting on the complete KPIs on the posture of each value driver is critical and should reflect in both cost and revenue synergy plans.

In Summary

- Understand complexity from every vantage point i.e., executive, mid manager, frontline troops, etc.
- Understand, dimension, and document good vs bad complexity.
- Make sure to not fall into the complexity "doom loop" i.e., put in place processes that keep bad complexity out.
- Reducing the variability of everything is a start to reducing complexity.
- Leveraging technologies such as machine learning etc. can help you navigate complexity more efficiently – once you have complexity, costs will

eventually increase, and the speed of
business will slow down.

14

Customer Due Diligence

During transactions, we hear various
flavors of due diligence i.e., Financial,
Legal, Operational, Commercial,
Technology IT, and more recently
Customer. So, what took it so long for
customer due diligence to become a
mainstream area of assessment? The key
answer is that companies and investors
thought they already did look at
customers through the lenses of
commercial and financial due diligence,
this is now proving to be insufficient.
Customer diligence is focused on the
customer versus the market and industry
dynamics often captured in commercial
due diligence.

A quick explanation of similarities,
differences, and correlations between
various due diligence bodies of work is
outlined below.

Financial	Commercial	Customer	Operational
Assess financial and transaction risks; both buy and sell side	Ascertain macro level risks and opportunities; typically buy side (VDD for sell side in EU)	Evaluate functional risks and opportunities with revenue synergy as primary focus; both buy and sell side	Functional assessment of risks and opportunities weighted towards cost synergies; both buy and sell side
• Quality of earnings, working capital, revenue and margin trends • Customer concentration, price and volume • Revenue recognition • Customer and vendor contracts • Debt, cash and foreign currency • Regulatory requirements • Accounting	• Industry trends, market dynamics, macro level impact • Market size, share and growth drivers • Business model relevance • Competitive landscape; source and sustainability of advantage • Customer concentration • Pricing trends	• Front office functions i.e., Sales, Marketing, Products, Service, Pricing and Customer Experience etc. • Validation of revenue levers like brand, channels, products, voice of customer, ability to upsell, cross-sell etc. • Revenue synergy primary, but cost synergies considered favorable • Integration planning where applicable	• Back-office or Operational functions i.e., IT, Finance, Real Estate, HR, Supply Chain, Manufacturing etc. • Validation of operating KPIs e.g. spend, organization, productivity, network/footprint etc. • Cost synergy or optimization assessments • Integration planning where applicable

Figure 6: Customer Diligence vs Other Diligences

Given the customer is at the heart of
revenue growth and any transaction
aimed at revenue uplift, revenue
synergies, etc. needs to examine the
quality, lifetime value, security, and
strength of customers and the levers
driving them. During an integration
scenario, customer diligence quantifies
revenue synergies and identifies key levers
necessary to realize them.

Customer diligence uncovers the strength of customer relationships and their role in the value of the target. Focused analysis can unlock pre-and post-transaction value through both insight and foresight including perception (and quality) of its engagement with customers and likely growth trajectory of the target.

Uncovering any risk of customer churn, decline, or defection before transaction close can validate revenue projections, products, customer experience, account strength, and competitive position specific to the target's ability to execute (not be confused by the competitive position of product or brand uncovered in a CDD).

Proactive risk reduction through focused retention planning can protect and enhance value across the business and mitigating risks emerging from customer concentration to products, geographies, or business units.

Uncovering growth drivers and levers towards new customer acquisition can help inform the development of a better roadmap to capitalize on the growth potential of the business. The earlier the acquirer can get and document both risks and opportunities, the earlier one can plan for post-close risk mitigation.

Examining cross-functional dependencies (by customer) is critical to understand dependencies, risks, decisions, and mitigation plan creation.

Typical buy-side assessment scope includes areas mentioned below (a non-exhaustive list):

Sales and Marketing Functions

- Document buyer targets, behaviors, and product selection criteria by class, including supporting promotions and messaging.

- Understand current market/demography coverage.
- Acquire current Sales and Marketing plans, with R&R and rules of engagement, high-level organization, and OpEx.
- Perform the PAR analysis of bookings.
- Assess ability to execute based on KPI like quota achievement, win ratio, and baseline performance.
- Confirm robustness of the pipeline.
- Build revenue forecasts at given levels of confidence, identify risks and opportunities in the current sales plan.

Brand

- Understand Brand image from an outside-in perspective and document consistency and effectiveness.
- Understand brand complexities by documenting various brand extensions, categories, positions, and strategy

including brands to grow, support, re-allocate or divest.

- Document Brand impact on various customer segments, employees, shareholders, product, and channel partners
- Analyze existing Brand metrics such as awareness, equity, perception, and document market impact on revenue, profitability, and potential.

Customers
- Understand the customer perspective through an outside-in view leveraging Voice of Customer (VoC)
- Perform a robust customer segmentation across two key assessment areas:
- Strategic – customer need, key features, buyer behavior, circumstance
- Operational – demographic focus, market trends

- Review key customer areas including concentration, penetration, tenure, loyalty, customer satisfaction (C-SAT), and cost to serve.
- Identify opportunities to drive deeper customer penetration through up-selling and cross-selling.

Products
- Assess alignment of product to customer needs.
- Evaluate the impact of substitute products on the target's competitive positioning and competitions barriers to entry.
- Document and understand the overall product lifecycle, road maps, and relevance in the industry.
- Understand product's scalability, stability, and speed to market relative to the market.
- Analyze product profitability and identify opportunities to rationalize,

bundle, and reposition products where appropriate.

Channels

- Understand channel structure (dealer, distribution, resellers, direct, etc.)
- Evaluate channel performance and alignment with a go-to-market strategy.
- Assess product to channel fit.
- Evaluate channel efficiency, cost structure, reach, and effectiveness.
- Understand channel leverage and document cross-sell and up-sell potential.

Pricing

- Benchmark pricing across the industry regarding similar and substitute products
- Understand pricing trends, forecasts, and sensitivity regarding products, markets, and channels.

- Understand price synergies for driving up volumes, positioning premium brands/products, and niche segments.
- Evaluate possible factors and timing leading to price changes post-acquisition.

Organization

- Analyze organizational levers including headcount, location, organization structure, the span of control, and layers.
- Assess the current brand and sales culture of the Target organization.
- Review roles and responsibilities
- Identify linkages with other organizations.
- Analyze incentive structure and assess its ability to drive behaviors consistent with organizational goals and strategy.

Integration Planning

- Validate integration strategy, including revenue and cost synergies.

- Assess customer-centric initiatives, one-time costs, timing, and level of effort.
- Understand the ability to execute, probability of success, resource constraints, and skillsets.
- Review high-level customer communication plan.

Customer diligence can also be performed on the sell side, unlike Commercial Due Diligence (in the US, Europe has a VDD). Sell-side aspects focus on pipeline impact, unbundling sales from prior bundled products, brand impact, and risk to volume, velocity, and value of the pipeline, etc. One can easily understand revenue, EBITDA, and Enterprise Value at risk due to the drivers on the sell-side. Performing customer due diligence allows acquirers to better plan, protect, and realize value.

Given below are key considerations and issues for buy and sell-side customer due diligence:

Key Considerations for Buy-Side Diligence (Non-exhaustive list)

Customer Concentration Risk

- How diversified is the target's customer base?
- Is the target's customer base overlapping or complementary to that of the buyer?
- How secure are customer relationships? (Evaluate sample contracts to understand key terms, duration, pricing, etc. relative to industry standards)

Cross-Selling Opportunities

- Have cross-selling opportunities being identified, prioritized, and communicated to the integrated Salesforce?

- Is the sales organization aligned on cross-selling priorities?
- How effective is the current market or territory coverage model?
- Do sales incentives drive the right behavior?
- How can sales personnel turnover be prevented?

Product Bundling
- How will products be bundled, rationalized, or reconfigured to accommodate products from the target?
- Who will be involved in key product bundling and market alignment decisions?
- How will the product bundling strategy be implemented to drive time to market improvement?
- How is the product development pipeline aligned with the product bundling and go-to-market strategy?

- What is the impact of product bundle size, configuration, price, and its impact on the supply and demand equation of the combined company?

Go-to-Market Functions

- What are key considerations in brand protection to minimize the negative perception of acquirer and target customers?
- How will customer relationships be protected and enhanced through the integration process?
- Are brand, product, and channel in alignment to meet market needs?
- Is the customer service function scalable to support the combined product portfolio?

Key Considerations for Sell-Side Diligence (Non-exhaustive list)

Sell-Side Value Chain Disruption

- Is the business being sold adequately staffed and skilled to execute all customer-facing needs?
- Is the organization heavily reliant on any specific customer or partner for large volumes of business?
- Will there be a loss of key specialists or core competencies?

Pipeline Conversion

- How does the business to be sold off differentiate itself from competitors? (e.g., origination capability, intellectual property, cost, servicing platforms, distribution, etc.)
- How will the organization's sales function be affected by the transaction?
- Will the sale of this business impact the remaining organizations go to market strategy?

Service and Customer Experience Disruption

- Does the organization structure effectively support customer needs?
- How to protect the remaining organization's brand and minimize negative reception due to the sale?
- Which customer relationships must be protected or enhanced due to the transaction?

Dis-synergies

- Will there be future revenue leakage from the last customers?
- Will there be lost economics of scale related to shared services agreements for customer functions such as customer service, customer payments processing, etc.?

Contracts and Pricing

- What are the significant legal agreements in existence with customers, suppliers, partners, vendors, etc.?

- What parts of the business are regulated? Is the business serving highly regulated industries?
- What impact does pricing undergo due to disruption in volume-based contracts?

My clients have often told me that commercial due diligence is often too high level and stayed focused on TAM numbers, pricing trends, industry dynamics, and other structural forces enabling or inhibiting growth at a macro level. What acquirers now want is a more granular view shifting from structural to functional analysis of core drivers and barriers in the functions requiring review of Sales, Marketing, Pricing, CX, etc.

In the evolving deal landscape, Quality of Customer assessments needs to be performed as rigorously as Quality of Earnings.

15

Merger of Equals

A Merger of Equals, a concept I have never agreed with during my M&A career and many seasoned transaction veterans share my view. Yet, we hear this term so often in the media and through executive messaging. I have experienced there are no two companies created equal, hence this messaging has always been somewhat problematic for me personally. If you dimension a company by e.g., size, capabilities, market share, brand, products, executive talent, engineering talent, geographic reach, depth of penetration, etc., companies are never equal across all (or even some) dimensions. One of them will always have superior capabilities in one or more areas.

The messaging is further contaminated when over-cautious boards, enthusiastic management teams carry out this messaging based on just two factors usually i.e., revenue size and headcount being in ballpark ranges of each other. A merger of equals is also perception and PR-driven creating quality or inequality views despite who paid for it.

In a recent survey that my old firm conducted, corporate development and M&A integration executives did mention specifically that executives messaging MOE (Merger of Equals) were in the top 3-4 reasons for sub-optimal M&A integration.

Having experienced these situations a few times, here are thoughts and practices on how to handle the M&A integration during an MOE:

Direction of Momentum

Right from the due diligence and integration planning stages be clear that integration messaging will be "forward-looking and constructive", and focus will be on how we move forward together and not on "why we are different and who will change", it will be about "how we create a joint culture together". Exceptions being the non-negotiables, like private companies merging with public companies, make sure the zero-tolerance zones are clear to everyone and they are implemented. These are not items to be brushed aside like an HR initiative shoved under change management or put off as soft fluff. Thinking the problem will be solved can be value threatening, the businesses must live with this aspect for months and years to come. Hence addressing decision making must be business owned and HR facilitated, not the other way around.

Decision Making

Consensus slows decision-making. Create a structure and process for making, communicating, and acting on decisions by ensuring executives are visibly involved. Make the tough, yet transparent decisions quickly especially where synergies or personnel are involved. Communicate jointly to employees, customers, suppliers, regulators, channel partners with a unified vision of the rationale behind decisions and what lies ahead.

Value Driver Focus

Executives and integration Leaders must clarify that nothing will supersede or circumvent the transaction value drivers, these must be executed by navigating barriers and differences. Usually, differences in company operating models are made the excuses to resist change, on a specific client I was helping, the integration leaders applauded and rewarded the creativity of people to navigate cultural minefields and operational differences to execute transaction value drivers.

Culture

Focusing a lot on culture change is not helpful, understand the culture, be respectful to each other's but also leverage similarities to foster execution and differences to protect or navigate around. Culture can only be gradually shaped, not changed overnight, and defining a shared vision for value creation is critical. Have "two in a box" leaders (one from each company) to enable future operating models, incentivize them to succeed while operating cohesively, and recognize small victories such as key integration milestones.

Channel Partners

While companies focus on customers and employees a lot, they often ignore channel partners. Partners are the extended sales force of the company and cannot be alienated. Be upfront about channel conflicts and have a very transparent plan on addressing them. Also, when size is often the only dimension to measure equality, issues such as one company not relying on channels trivializes the other who does (common). This needs to be addressed at the due diligence itself, channel partners take the blame for not realizing revenue synergies. A leading practice is to have one or two channel partner workshops (early) and listen to what they have to say after you communicate the combined company vision, both companies should be represented in equal strength when these sessions occur. Do not send someone to just check the box.

Avoid the Traps of Resistance

Understand patterns of resistance and not fall into the traps of delays or fighting change. I have seen five distinct patterns of resistance i.e., unnecessary uniqueness, a culture of democracy, infinite appeals, justified delays, and technical flamethrowers - more on these in another article. But plan to counter these patterns and develop foresight on mitigation plans without upsetting the apple cart. Transactions positioned as MOE are sometimes very emotional and about egos; one must reinforce positive tones and lots of energy even if people resist. Be prepared to quickly move out people slowing down the process through elevated patterns of change resistance while rewarding people who embrace speed and change.

The most successful integrations (well relatively) after messaging "merger of equals" had some of these characteristics:

- Strong sense of who was more capable in what area.
- A clear understanding of non-negotiables, full transparency on degrees of execution freedom.
- Strong "two in a box" integration leadership - incentivized for teaming, creative navigation of barriers, and hitting integration milestones.
- Combined culture definition, as opposed to a culture integration.
- Integration being themed around "forward-looking and constructive."

At the risk of repeating myself, there is no such thing as a merger of equals and no two companies are equal across all material dimensions. I would continue to advise executives and boards to refrain from open messaging around "merger of equals". If any of you fall victim to the MOE messaging, hope some of these above-mentioned guidelines could help.

16

M&A Integration: Creating Value from High-priced Tuck-ins

The Landscape Today

Transactions today are complex; technology innovation and disruption are making the valuations of small companies appear big and that of big companies appear small. Today, small-sized targets are neither small on price nor complexity; value needs to deliver by integrating differently, given synergies do not exist conventionally. These so-called 'tuck-in' acquisitions protect or enhance the underlying economic logic in the buyer's industry and purchase high purchase prices are a norm. Investors are demanding quicker ROI and there is pressure on the executives to deliver transaction value. The 2014 acquisition of WhatsApp (<5 years old, 55 employees, last VC funding value was at $1.5 billion) by Facebook for $19 billion is a classic example - investors were so skeptical over the deal creating value >$19 billion affecting a share price drop of 5%.

Challenges with Tuck-in Value Creation

The size of these companies typically creates underinvestment in areas like IT and other back-office functions considered conventional sources of cost synergy, making revenue growth the primary value creation play. Most organizations have been through cost reduction, reengineering, restructuring, and countless other cost optimization projects, whether they were triggered by M&A or otherwise. These are known game plans, with an experience base to build on. Revenue synergies are often more dependent on variables requiring new skills, new methods, new products or services, new channels, or even a new business model. Delivering revenue synergies with 'tuck-ins' requires buy-in from the target company and rapid ability to rally align your customer segment, brand, channels, and sales force backing the new value proposition. Integrating for value requires a different approach than conventional functional integration.

Integration Strategies for Tuck-ins
Product-Centric

Acquiring companies leave products standalone after the acquisition leaving and often leaking value. There are several ways of integrating products for value and they center on understanding the source and sustainability of product during the diligence, creating a product road map for preserving key elements of value, and enhancing other areas such as portfolio fit and profitability by day one. Create opportunities for product bundling, rationalizing products or features quickly, and understand opportunities for new product development as a long-term play. Bundles and pricing can drive a lot of incremental value if executed well.

User Value Centric
The new lever in the era of user, content, and data monetization enabling a variety of business models from advertising, subscriptions, x-selling, up-selling, etc. Total users and active users present unique sources of value. In Facebook's case, the market eventually recognized that with WhatsApp's >450 million active mobile users and rapid user growth, Facebook was acquiring a potentially formidable competitor and strengthening its mobile position simultaneously. The price paid for WhatsApp was ~$42 per mobile user and ~3.5x less than the market placed on each mobile user of Facebook itself ($141) or Twitter ($124).

Understanding the key attributes of user data, its value by segment, and monetization potential should inform the integration plan.

Channel Centric
Channels or routes to market are key value drivers, and certain products are well suited to specific channels. As a new product is embedded into the portfolio, leveraging the buyer's channel for scale, or reaching new customer segments is critical. A key aspect to delivering value is to make sure that customer segments, brand, products, and pricing align quickly to support the channel early in the transaction cycle and clear barriers such as channel conflicts, efficiencies, and carry factors.

Talent Centric
Tuck-ins come with two clear value plays i.e., product (or technology) and talent (acqui-hires, the industry name for it),

success of one without the other is questionable but the major difference is that talent-centric transactions are originated from product teams (usually not corporate development) and talent can be reassigned to work in various parts of the business despite the target's product. Retaining these individuals is key and cultural diligence early on helps identify risks with talent including implications on talent strategy, retention planning, career paths, integrating stay incentives, and risks of alienating existing talent. Acceleration opportunities for products, go to market, impact on recruiting budgets, etc. need to be measured rigorously to capture and report the value to shareholders.

As the velocity of disruption increases and the war for talent intensifies, the volume and value of tuck-in acquisitions will continue to rise with investors demanding more transparency and quicker returns. This will get acquiring organizations to rethink their integration playbooks and conventional view on synergies.

17

M&A Integration: Customer Experience (CX) as a Value Driver

Over the last few years, M&A has become a top-line growth play in many sectors making customers the center of focus during integration between two companies. Acquirers have evolved from defensive plays around customer retention to aggressive customer acquisition, proactive predatory plays on new customer segments leveraging acquired capabilities and enhancing customer experience. While CX (Customer Experience) has evolved into a well-defined body of knowledge, its application in the M&A context is often not well understood. In the last few transactions, I have done, my clients have explicitly requested assistance and advice with CX with full work streams swinging into action with the IMO.

There are several aspects to CX as a value driver and is integral to other levers of value such as Brand, Channels, Products, Customer Segments, etc.

Core Objectives of CX during M&A Integration

- Preserve (existing) and enhance (develop new) customer experience through disciplined execution M&A Integration
- Drive customer acquisition, retention, brand strategy, and loyalty by providing distinctive customer experiences through focused CX integration.
- Make enhanced customer experience a catalyst to drive revenue synergies utilizing key levers such as branding (premium positioning), products (enriched experience and creating

stickiness), pricing (pay for value), customer segments (penetrating new customers), and channels (generating additional pull)

CX Transaction Considerations

All customer touchpoints from both companies require careful attention, the interaction model at each touchpoint needs to be understood for where it needs to be preserved and what needs to be enhanced. Each customer segment values interaction model(s) differently and hence mapping them to the right customer segment is critical.

Besides considering CX being its workstream, embedding it into all ancillary work streams is a leading practice area touching sales, marketing, service, and support.

CX can be positively or negatively affected due to changes in policies, operational processes, or systems. Anticipating the neutral and negative experiences of key customers or customer segments will help design safety nets against dissatisfaction or flight risks; typical components of safety nets include promotions, targeted incentives, executive coverage, and operationalizing exception management processes.

Before Day One, ensure there is adequate infrastructure, systems, and training to support the target customer experience. This must be remarkably high on the priority list during Integration Planning.

Use product bundling, packaging, and delivery and key levers for enhancing CX; train sales, marketing, and service to position, communicate, and sell CX as a key differentiator.

Understand, document, measure, and report customer experience across all functions such as Sales, Marketing, Service, Support, Product Development, R&D Billing, and Invoicing

Customer experience is not a nebulous thing in today's age, it has a significant impact on transaction value realization and can be analyzed and executed in a very actionable, measurable, and tactical manner. Treating CX as a value driver or workstream can benefit the overall transaction value realization.

18

M&A Brand Integration

The search for revenue growth is now becoming a core driver behind M&A making revenue synergies or GTM synergies an especially important part of deal value.

Marketing (along with Sales) becomes the central force driving revenue and profitability while being closest to the customers. Yet, integrating the marketing function is not given its due in M&A integration - a recent survey from FTI Consulting revealed Marketing being of strategic importance but lesser resources dedicated towards M&A integration.

There are multiple areas to address within Marketing from an M&A integration standpoint, a non-exhaustive list is outlined below:

Brand Strategy

Managing the entire portfolio of multiple brands, creating a new brand architecture from existing brands while aligning and creating a new value proposition. Understanding brand health, brand awareness, and brand equity, possibly divesting weaker brands

Product Strategy

Rationalizing the product portfolio in alignment with branding strategy, evaluating pricing, and setting them in alignment with new markets, products, and brands; determining target markets, customer segments, product proposition, and positioning.

Customer Retention

Reassuring existing customers; executing effective retention programs and promotions.

Communications Strategy and Channel Enablement

Communicating new branding and enabling channel partners; ensuring channels (including digital) are aligned to brand strategy; press and public relations to optimize shareholder value.

Marketing Organization

Aligning new organization structure and skills; selecting leadership; defining incentives, KPIs, and retaining talent looking across all levers like headcount, spans, and layers and locations to optimize organization design.

Synergies

Identifying critical levers to drive market growth to meet analyst and company expectations such as new customer segments, new channels, and new capabilities enabling revenue synergies. Execute cost synergies from headcount, systems, tools, and contracts by rationalizing where applicable.

Marketing and Campaign Operations

Effectively leveraging scale to achieve operational efficiencies, managing agency relationships across multiple brands.

The more successful acquirers take a holistic and deep approach to the integration of Marketing as opposed to a peripheral view limited to individuals and incentives.

To create value from Marketing, companies need to have a holistic view of the entire GTM ecosystem, details around touchpoints, products portfolio, lead generation, conversion velocity, account marketing support, marketing operations coverage pricing, contracts, products, and customer service. Open communication (at the executive level) to customers creates trust, openness, sets the tone for

their needs and expectations, and creates
new allies in the success of the
transaction.

Strategies	Attributes	Perspective	Pros	Cons
Brand Centric	• Overall brand strategy • Brand value and value • Brand Purpose • Culture	Brand ambiguity can be one of the three inhabiting the short term brand, incorporating elements from both organizational or building a new brand	No radical changes to the brand that worked well in the past and act a strong platform	Brand decisions often tend to have developmental biases and could send mixed messages. Risks can be seen, potential insights are that could cut Brand with the end-objective lose ground integration.
Performance Centric	• Historical performance • Market shifts and trends • Market share and lead conversion • Channel performance • Culture	Historical data is used as a baseline to determine future state	Analytics and data driven approach and offers success on a single trajectory of growth	Historical baselines need to be usable cautious like towards transformation efforts
Customer Centric	• Breadth and depth of relationship • Customer loyalty • Needs and opportunity driven	Objective of introducing new products and services to serve new or some needs within customer segments	Customer insights and relationships are driven toward and increase penetration with an existing and new customers	Focus tends to be too much on executive facing, front-office activities and backend processes often are ignored
Product Centric	• Product synergies • Channel synergies • Partner ecosystem	Serving existing customers through more efficient product/services mix or reaching new customers through newly acquired channels	Product centric approach can be instrumental in generating quick wins as well enhancing brand focus	Managing product portfolios, channels and customer needs long term vision and commitment

Figure 7: Strategies for Marketing and Brand Integration

An M&A Marketing Integration strategy
once selected should be translated into an
operational framework that not only
includes everything needing to be
accomplished in terms of depth and
breadth but also focuses on weightage,
priority, sequence, and level of rigor based
on the transaction specificities and value
drivers.

19

Org Design in New Business Model M&A

In today's era of rapid business model disruption, conventional approaches to M&A integration are also being disrupted and new paradigms of preserving and enhancing value are emerging. Integrating new business models involves several differences in how one should think about making the new organization work, based on my experiences in the TMT (Tech, Media, and Telecom) sectors, the following are key considerations while thinking through the organizational design of the new company.

Examine Decision Levers

Integrating new business models is always a challenge, the new organization is a core value driver, and get this right. Specific decision levers include keeping organizations separate in the short term, combining them quickly, or using an overlay approach. Decisions should be driven based on data and facts looking at the impact on brands, channels, markets, and products, another consideration for organizational design is the potential of one business to cannibalize the other e.g., SaaS and perpetual licensing business models can conflict with each other, SDN will cannibalize the existing MPLS business of Telcos, hence these issues need to be carefully addressed with clear answers in place by Day One.

Sequence Matters

Once the executive layers of the company are announced, the second level needs to quickly be put in place. When integrating new business models like IoT, SaaS, SDN, etc., it is almost a given that the value is carried by the product, the people, and the brand hence making these the top 3 areas of focus. In a transaction where the product is driving the core value, design that organization first and then create linkages into marketing/brand integration, then sales whether overlay or not with the right incentives in a very specific sequence considering all risks and dependencies. Due care must be taken to not mimic the legacy business model benchmarks on spans, layers, locations, etc. preserving the differences. The operational systems such as lead to cash and HR must support the new business model by not taking the homogeneity view.

Manage Executive Repatriation

One needs to pay specific attention to the skills and background of acquired executives. It is getting increasingly common to see people get to titles like Vice Presidents in large traditional organizations and then transition into smaller start-ups with similar titles. While larger organizations tend to "title down" several people from start-ups when calibrating them against the size, span, and job complexity of the acquirer, specific attention needs to be given to the people who had marched up the executive ranks in prior jobs based on their caliber and experience. Under-titling them could lay a platform for discontentment and ultimately departure.

Culture Integration

The new business culture alignment approach focuses on creating a "new way" together. Typically, it is delivered by energizing leaders and managers through offsite summits by brainstorming the future state rather than an assessment of each other's cultures. Critical success factors include strengths-based teamwork, developing relationships, genuine connections, sparking ideas, and driving ownership. The approach is gaining more adoption and faster delivery of results in M&A integration, with more focus on culture alignment than homogenizing.

No Incentives, No Progress

Like everything else, homogenizing incentives will create a business drag. Given the inherent difference in the business models, one needs to align individual and group incentives with the core KPIs about the new business model (not the legacy business). Three C's need to be addressed:

Commitment

Are the incentives really in place and is leadership committed to delivering on the committed plans?

Cohesion

Are the incentives going to propel the joint company forward by fostering people working together?

Conflict

Is there a conflict of incentive structures between business models? Done to remove any inherent tensions between the business models to prevent cannibalization?

As disruptive technologies continue to emerge and impact existing business models, legacy companies will rely on M&A as a driver to transition their businesses. Integrating new business models differs vastly from looking at traditional transactions involving consolidations, tuck-ins, or even adjacencies, and getting the organization's design is imperative for maximizing value from these transactions.

20

M&A Integration Governance Models

We have come a long way from the pure consolidation or diversification types of deals prevalent in the 1980s and 90s, even the first part of the century witnessed some of these. In today's world we have a fair share of consolidations and adjacency diversifications, to add to it we have high volumes of technology tuck-ins, acquihires, carve-out integrations, and new business model acquisitions. In 2019 and 2020, deal volume, velocity, and values attained record levels and some buyers did deals across all categories creating a lot more integration complexity.

M&A integration approaches have changed over the last 3-4 years, today's deals demand a very custom approach. Changes have materially affected the design of IMO, workstream configurations, key metrics, governance models, and new ways of thinking about synergies and shareholder value.

This chapter will focus on various governance models that can be considered during an M&A integration. Just like a rigid IMO structure does not scale across all deal types; governance models need to be adapted to maximize deal value. Remember if IMO is tasked with flying the plane, the governance is the air traffic control - particularly important to keep in sync.

Based on my several years of serving clients and experience with nearly a thousand deals, I have come up with a few distinct governance models, see figure below.

Selecting governance models are based on a few important criteria; a non-exhaustive list is below:

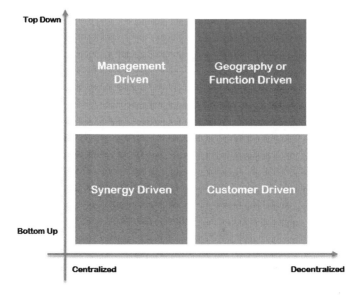

Figure 8: Governance Frameworks for M&A Integration

- **Deal Type:** primary value drivers e.g., cost, revenue, capability, etc.
- **Primary Sponsors/Stakeholders:** whose interests are being served and who should have decision rights.

- **Organization Structure:** corporate versus geographic alignment, executive proximity, and level of engagement with customers and employees
- **Culture:** product vs customer vs sales-oriented organization, whether this can be an accelerator or barrier to value
- **IMO Configuration:** functional approach versus value driver configuration of workstreams, the posture of IMO e.g., drive and deliver versus lead and influence, etc.
- **Strategic Rationale:** gain scale, gain specific capability, pre-emptive strike, hostile takeover, transform business model, etc.

The right governance model has proved to be an accelerator of value creation, in prior years focus was always on protecting the value and enabling transparency with stakeholders. M&A leaders need to think a lot more about putting the right governance model and IMO posture in

place to unlock more value. After all, one cannot expect to create value by using yesterday's playbooks for tomorrow's deals.
There are typical situations when each of these governance models makes sense with associated pros and cons, all this needs to be evaluated through the criteria mentioned above.

The factors at play and the deal itself will determine the selection criteria of the optimal governance model, this is part art and part science. The governance model, the IMO posture, and the deal type are critical to getting aligned to create value.

Governance Model	Typical Situation	Pros	Cons
Top Down and Centralized	• Business model or business strategy centric deal • Executives understand the criticality of business model transition; heavier board involvement	• Maintain executive oversight, create transparency and reinforce criticality • Board members care about shareholder value rather than synergies • IMO is directly responsible for synergies	• Can be too distant from products and/or customers and decision making will be difficult • Synergies not mapped to specific shareholder value metrics will be difficult to articulate
Bottom Up and Centralized	• M&A integration strategy based approach • Synergies are identified in specific functions largely cost synergies • Prior experience executing several similar deals	• IMO leader driven, classic playbook approach on proven and tested process and metrics • Finite cost, from defines functions, well understood cost levers, tolls and KPIs • Functional workstreams responsible for synergies in full control supported by IMO	• Does not scale to revenue synergy or new business model deals where products, customers and value driver configuration is at play • IMO runs the process, but strategy and operations skillsets create value • Not being close to the business, customers and products can add risk
Top Down and Centralized	• Used for efficiency • Functional leaders directly responsible for synergies	• Tighter governance on larger deals, single center of accountability • Maintains seamless vertical and horizontal flow of information • Experiences IMOs in full control supported by functional workstreams	• Can get very complex if run top down or bottom up alone; needs to have a full RACI on a deal to deal basis • Will not scale to decentralized and autonomous organizations (buyer or target)
Bottom Up and Decentralized	• Used for effectiveness • Synergies come from multiple functions and revenue synergies are centered around specific customers • Product, sales and regional teams are closest to customers as compared to executives	• Has a very customer centric approach and value creating teams are typically in charge • Value driver configuration for IMOs as opposed to typical functional plays; value creation is primary objective • Value driver workstream leads in full control ; IMO plays augment and report role	• Has more moving parts, inexperienced IMOs or purely process centric IMOs will create execution risk • Model not suitable to be governed by personnel distant from business, products or customers • Bottom up configuration yields optimal results, at times conflicts with management traditional top down approach

Figure 9: Governance Models Overview

M&A integration today is not about rigid processes and playbooks as priorities shift from managing the integration process to creating value. It is all about pattern recognition and aligning the right governance model with the right deal pattern.

21

M&A Integration of Sales Channels

The Sales function encompasses multiple sub-areas such as account management, field sales, sales operations, inside sales, channels, avoiding channel conflicts, etc. Channels help increase market coverage and enable companies to compete globally. There are different channel partners e.g., direct resellers, distributors, system integrators, etc.

Managing and effectively integrating channels can be a source of both cost and revenue synergy. Channels contribute to roughly 66% of the sales in the Technology sector today, it has grown more than double digits over the last 5 years. It continues to grow in other industries as ecosystems develop and mature.

The channel integration planning phase itself needs to consider implications of immediate combination, staged integration, and leaving certain aspects as is. A consolidated channel structure, channel partner tiers, contracts, sales processes, data management from POS, CRM systems, sales compensation, and incentives are big factors in how stability is achieved, and synergies are delivered.

Seven specific areas need to be thought through in an M&A Integration:

Focus Area	Value Driver	Synergy Type
Account Management	• Governance and cadence • Overlapping accounts • Harmonize processes and tools • Partner selection and onboarding process • Consistency of NPI (new product introduction)	Cost and Revenue
Partner Margins	• Protecting differentiation and distribution • Avoiding channel conflicts	Cost
Managing Contra Revenue	• Harmonizing incentive structures • Unified contra tracking at program and channel level • Optimizing and integrating contra spend (demand gen vs inventory vs partner incentive); ensure compliance on MDF	Cost
Targets and Programs	• New target opportunities, optimize existing targets • Align channel to combined product portfolio	Cost and Revenue
Coverage and Skills	• Coverage model e.g., gaps, overlap and leverage • Optimize mix of generalists vs specialists	Cost and Revenue
Quoting	• Integrate pricing based on tiers, channels and products • Unified quote to cash view of combined co. • Protect and enhancing TAT on pricing quotes • Consistency in workflows and handoffs	Cost and Revenue
Data Management	• Timely data from POS • Integrated and agreed upon taxonomy • Data governance, KPIs and operations	Cost

Figure 10: Typical Areas of Sales Assessment

Sales Channel Integration: Key Questions

- How is the acquired company's channel organization (channel sales, sales admin, and partner operations) structured?
- What is the headcount by function/process area?
- What are the functions supported by the partner operations organization? What are the similarities and differences?

- Are there other channel activities managed elsewhere? e.g., partner training, channel marketing, etc.?
- What is the partner coverage model? 1:1 Channel Business Manager assignment or group assignment by partner membership level/tier?
- What is the channel operating model? Gold, silver, bronze, etc.
- Do partners stock? (Not applicable for most enterprise software sales and XaaS sales)
- What percentage of channel sales are drop-shipped? (Not applicable for most enterprise software sales and XaaS sales)
- What is the partner management cadence and structure? How is it different by partner tier?
- What is the list of partners (including Distributors) along with sell-in and sale-out data for the past few completed quarters?

- How does the partner list of the acquired company map to that of the acquiring company?
- How is partner sales goal attainment managed?
- How is the partner compensation matrix managed? Is it by product line or flat across product lines?
- How is the channel program structured? What are the key elements of the channel program? Is it a single umbrella program or a collection of small programs?
- How is MDF planned, managed, and disbursed?
- How are partner agreements managed? Do all partners have a partnership agreement with the company or are it only applicable to the distributors and other direct buying partners (like Direct Market Resellers, System Integrators, etc.)? Are the

- partner agreements evergreen or do they expire after a certain duration?
- What are the different partner types? How do they map to that of the acquiring company?
- Are partner relationships managed locally at the country level or are they managed globally?

Most organizations give a lot of attention to their customers and employees and rightly so — the area of channels is often overlooked. Integrating channels effectively is necessary from a value protection (compliance, conflicts, etc.), value capture (cost synergies), and new value creation (revenue synergies) standpoint. A lot needs to fall in place by day one itself, bringing channel partners into the integration fold can go a long way in retaining channel partners, retaining key employees, improving product positions, and penetration while adding new partners.

22

M&A Sales Integration Strategy

One of the biggest challenges during M&A is the integration of Salesforces. Sales (along with Marketing) is the central force driving revenue and profitability while being closest to the customers. Yet, integrating sales forces and retaining personnel ranks amongst the top risks in M&A — a recent survey from FTI Consulting revealed that the Sales function had 3X more turnover than the average.

The more successful acquirers take a holistic and deep approach to the integration of Sales as opposed to a peripheral view limited to individuals and incentives. To create value from Sales, companies need to have a holistic view of customer relationships by Salesperson, details around customer touchpoints, products sold, inventory velocity, account management support, sales operations coverage, pricing, contracts, delivery, and customer service. Open communication (at the executive level) to customers creates trust, openness, sets the tone for their needs and expectations, and creates new allies in the success of the transaction. Channels include routes to market selling products and services through a network of distributors, resellers, and agents/influencers who are critical stakeholders in the transaction, they are often ignored with the focus being on customers and employees — getting them on board is important and can be pivotal to the success and failure of the sales integration.

There are principally four integration strategies with Sales integration, refer to the table below:

Strategies	Attributes	Perspective	Pros	Cons
Capability Centric	• Organization • Structure and roles • Sales coverage and focus • Sales force deployment • Culture	Typically based on acquirer and target's self evaluation of these dimensions	No radical changes in areas and capabilities that worked well in the past, changes are more surgical based on newly acquired capabilities	Capability decisions made by employees often tend to have pre-acquisition biases and could create conflict
Performance Centric	• Historical performance • Market shifts and trends • Market share and profitability • Channel performance • Sales growth • Culture	Historical data is used as a baseline to determine future state	Analytics and data driven approach and often focused on a single trajectory of growth	Historical baselines tend to be counterproductive towards transformation efforts
Customer Centric	• Breadth and depth of relationship • Customer loyalty • Needs and opportunity driven • Coverage Models	Driven by cross-sell, up-sell potential, coverage model and the opportunity to introduce new products serving unmet needs	Customer insights and relationships can drive focus and increase penetration within existing and new customer segments	Focus tends to be too much on customer facing, front-office activities and backend processes often times are ignored
Channel Centric	• Product synergies • Channel cost • Partner ecosystem	Serving existing customers through more efficient channels or reaching new customers through newly acquired channels	Channels are partner centric approach can be instrumental in generating quick wins and rapid scale for new products	Managing channels and partners needs long term vision, engagement, incentives and commitment i.e., not just a few days after the transaction

Figure 11: Sales Integration Strategies

An M&A Sales Integration strategy once
selected should be translated into a
tactical operational framework that not
only includes everything needing to be
accomplished in terms of depth and
breadth but also focuses on weightage,
priority, sequence, and level of rigor based
on the transaction specificities and value
drivers.

23

M&A Integration Value from Go-to-Market Functions

M&A Integration surveys have revealed that more organizations are now seeking revenue growth as opposed to cost reduction through M&A. At the heart of revenue growth is the customer and therefore functions that touch customers such as sales, marketing, service, products, customer experience and pricing on the front end and customer service, billing, invoicing, and collections at the back end become critical to align and integrate a right way to maintain stability or develop a sustainable competitive advantage.

Yet, several companies fall short of harnessing revenue synergies as integration teams get caught harnessing quick hits through back-office consolidations and leave revenue synergies aside. Synergies from customer-facing functions are more transformative and take longer to realize, they could also require upfront investments counter-intuitive to the rapid cost reductions that organizations are so used to executing. Ensuring revenue continuity lays a good platform for executing growth.

When an organization acquires revenue, it is one or more of the four out of the four levers i.e., brands, channels, new customer segments, or products, and often one of them is a primary driving force. Whichever be the primary driver, the other three need to align to it quickly. For example, if a product is a primary driver - the channel structure, target customer segments, and the brand need to rally behind it soon.

Four primary strategies towards GTM integration can be leveraged to maximize revenue synergies, each requires a multitude of different skills to be in focus when executing for success.

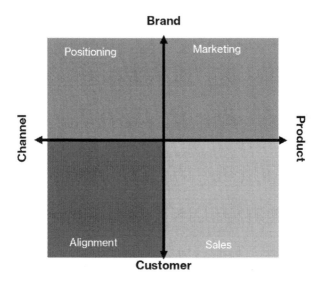

Figure 12: GTM Integration Framework

Brand Centric
Skills around sales/marketing, positioning, messaging, and culture of relationship building.

Customer-Centric

Skills around data/analytics and culture of decisiveness, customer engagement, and collaboration.

Channel Centric
Skills cost/efficiency leverage and culture of continuous improvement.

Product-Centric
Skills on innovation/features, portfolio alignment, and culture of empowerment

	Typical Deal Concerns	Day 1 (Protecting Value)	Day 100 (Capturing Value)	Longer Term (Creating Value)
Brand	Protection	Messaging and communication	Redefinition an alignment	Rebranding
Product	Dilution	Portfolio fitment, product road Maps and profitability	Product bundling, product rationalization and pricing changes	New product development and product innovation
Channel	Confusion	Mitigate channel conflict, call my channel optimization an alignment with product and customer segments	Increase effectiveness; rationalize, reconfigure and realign	New channel acquisition or channel transformation
Customer	Retention	Customer segmentation, profitability assessments and retention planning	Drop unprofitable customers, cross sell and upsell to more profitable customers	Selling new products to new customers

Figure 13: Typical GTM Value Drivers

Typical M&A integration issues related to the GTM functions

Brand Protection

Acquisitions are *rarely* done to switch brands; they are mostly undertaken to fill the product or service gaps within existing portfolios. Hence having a pervasive brand strategy makes sure that everyone is aligned on the execution. The Brand elevation for the combined entity should be the primary goal and organizations should not get caught in the misguided efforts to preserve the acquired company's brand beyond a certain point, these misguided efforts have a huge drain on resources in the functions that should be driving growth and confuse the customers. Products and channels must change and change quickly to fit the brand strategy so this can lay a platform for growth.

Customer Retention
Customers are at the heart of the revenue growth strategy and no organization can derive revenue synergies without them.

Each customer or account either lost or diminished makes it that much more difficult to attain revenue synergies. Maintaining transparency with customers, articulating value early and clearly, not overselling, keeping performance high, and integrating customer-related activities at the end when the rest of the infrastructure is in place is core to the integration strategy. Some of the critical activities that should be taken upfront are to design a safety net for the customers under flight risk, these are typically customers affected negatively by changes in policies, operational processes, or systems that will downgrade their experiences, the safety net can be a set of activities that include promotions, targeted incentives, exception management protocols, and executive-level coverage. Incentivizing the sales force to retaining customers is also overly critical to success. A favorable outcome of good channel integration is to generate customer pull than product push.

Channel Confusion

Channels are a way to reach the customers most efficiently and effectively, they can be an integral part of the customer experience. Many times, during mergers acquiring new channels and integrating them is the end game. Channels need to be in harmony with the brand and products. The alignment between Sales, Marketing, Channels, Products, and Customer segments being in perfect harmony is the only way to capitalize on revenue synergies, this also needs to be done rather quickly after the basic functions and infrastructure are in place, products are rationalized, and mapped to the right channels in line with the brand strategy.

Product Dilution

Products must fit the overall portfolio and align with the brand strategy. This would include names, packaging, look and feel which impact the customer experience. Having a framework to name, position, integrate, and communicate about products and their value propositions early on is a key to success. Duplicate and competing products must be rationalized, and the sales force must clearly understand the value drivers in the new product portfolio and how is aligned. Integrating and mapping the right products to the right channels is vital to realize cross-sell and upsell opportunities by hitting the right target customer segments.

People and Culture Integration

Culture at a high level can be defined as *'the way of doing things*, after every M&A integration activity there does occur a culture shift, however, it needs to be controlled and aligned with the vision and goals of the organization and its leadership. Business leaders must recognize the culture required to drive the shift and place a lot of emphasis on the right organizational design and incentives that will align the right behaviors with the desired results. M&A often identifies cultural similarities but overlooks cultural differences which make integration challenging. Culture and change succeed when business is owned, and HR facilitated and not the other way around as typically witnessed in many organizations.

Getting Tactical

Some examples of value drivers and tactical considerations (non-exhaustive list) from the GTM functions which help create value from GTM functions:

Strategy and Business Model

- Review the alignment of go-to-market and business strategy (product, channel, brand, market, customer segments, key relationships, etc.)
- Understand the source and sustainability of existing competitive advantage in potential multipliers.
- Evaluate cultural similarities and differences in the selling model and roadblocks to success.

Key Accounts

- Identify top accounts, value drivers, and assess future opportunities.
- Identify accounts that are underserved due to capacity constraints or lack of coverage.
- Evaluated the risk-adjusted opportunity to better penetrate for cross-selling and upselling.
- Identify and quantify unprofitable accounts.

- Evaluate contractual commitments and termination constraints.

Customers

- Identify top customers, overall customer concentration, level of one-time versus repeat business, and cost to serve.
- Evaluate key buying criteria and measure performance against these criteria.
- Assess customer satisfaction KPI's, frequency of metrics publishing key personnel/organization in charge of customer satisfaction.

Products/Services

- Evaluate the profitability of products and service offerings.
- Identify potential rationalization and consolidation opportunities as a combined company.
- SS product fitment for overall brand strategy and positioning

- Understand channel alignment of each future state product and service.

Marketing
- Evaluate lead generation and lead routing practices to identify value opportunities.
- Evaluate overlapping marketing efforts and expenses.
- Identify marketing commitments and termination clauses like trade shows print media etc.
- Quantify the potential of streamline marketing efforts, certain services provided by the parent, and associated cost allocations.

Integration Planning
- Assess the overall customer and channel integration strategy, identify revenue associated with the integrated state.

- Analyze the key integration initiatives, including one-time costs, timing, and level of effort.
- Understand factors such as the probability of success, resource constraints, and conflicting initiatives affecting timing for growth realization.

Sales
- Assess the risk-adjusted opportunity based on historical experience, projected e.g., selling a new product to an existing customer, selling into a greenfield customer, etc. Correlate with market structure, customer needs, and segment growth
- Quantify future opportunities based on salesforce realignment, territory, product, and channel coverage; Look for rationalization opportunities.
- Identify gaps in incentive alignment.

Pricing

- Understand historic pricing trends, price elasticity, and forecast for prices in the near term.
- Understand supply constraints, price sensitivity to growing volumes, and projected synergies.
- Understand pricing strategy; For example, should the price be raised for certain customer segments, or should they be lowered to drive up volume and capture market share.

At all given times, brand, product, channel, customer segments, and culture must stay aligned in total sync. An organization pursuing any strategy eventually needs to align and integrate other drivers but using one as the starting point is the winning strategy.

24

Acquiring Disruptive Business Models

The rules of business continue to be redefined by disruptive technologies, and at a global scale altering business models, value propositions, customer needs, interaction models, the economic logic for underlying profits, and the evolution of new, interconnected ecosystems.

The changes are more so in the last 3-4 years. There is disruption everywhere with technologies like Cloud, Software Defined Everything, Open Source, Artificial Intelligence, IoT, Blockchain and Augmented/Virtual Reality, etc. going mainstream and creating new business models across many industries. Older and more established players must reinvent themselves or be displaced into oblivion.

All this has changed the thinking behind how M&A strategy is conceptualized and executed i.e., integration. The very questions around the definition of value and how to maximize it has gone through a big shift e.g., what areas to focus on during due diligence? Which synergies does one focus on? How does one create value? etc.

Strategy is Hard, M&A Strategy is Harder

The Tech sector was the disruptor for the early part of this century and today it is also disrupted. A lot of older and legacy technology companies missed the new paradigms and are seeking to acquire themselves out of the disrupted business models by acquiring newer technologies and enabling business models. The number of shifts in control points that companies must deal with is non-trivial today, the shifting controls are conflicting and hence make strategy definition and formulation a lot more difficult than prior years. Some examples of these business model changing technology shifts are:

- Hardware to Software
- License to Cloud
- Cloud to Edge
- Centralized to Decentralized.
- Decentralized to Centralized.
- Human to Machine
- Real to Virtual
- Voice to Data
- Data to Voice
- Closed to Open.
- Enterprise to Ecosystem

Which tech strategy to back? What is a winning business model? What to acquire? Where is the risk etc.? These are all difficult questions to answer in today's dynamic and uncertain environment.

Impact on M&A Strategy and Due Diligence

All these shifts have affected the very thinking behind M&A strategy through integration, a quick look at the key changes:

- It is more challenging for companies to approach a new business model, as it is out of their traditional realm of doing business. For example, selling licensed software and SaaS have different economics, KPIs, and go-to-market approaches.
- Typically, the older (or new) model cannibalizes the new (or older) model making GTM decisions a lot harder.
- There are no conventional synergies to realize from back offices, life is all about product and revenue synergies for the most part.
- Disruptive technologies or capabilities are not just one thing, putting clear definitions on an array of required

capabilities and their impact requires heavier alignment between corporate strategy and corporate development.

- Culture due diligence and Technology (not IT) diligence ascertaining source and sustainability of value become critical.
- Single acquisitions never materially transform business models, developing a view of assets in combination to foster a pipeline with an invigorated level of engagement with the target companies is more important than ever.
- Defensive vs Offensive plays need to be differentiated; the former is more dilutive.

Impact on Valuation

Traditional valuations on multiple EBITDA, DCF, etc. have broken down with valuations trending much higher making it harder to articulate this to boards and investors.

Many of my clients now feel that acquiring disruptive assets is expensive and harder to justify on valuation, value also means the direct impact on the equity profile or stock price. Markets would take better to an acquisition strategy that is cohesive and messages to acquisition leading to a higher value business model. In my experience we have four types of value-adding deals well received by markets:

Catalyst Transactions: The first acquisition signaling acquirers intent to change and embark on embracing change and think about the future.

Strengthen the Stack: Specific capabilities like AI. Cyber, analytics, etc. which enhance the posture of the existing value chain and can lay the foundation for future acquisitions.

Creating Competitive Advantage:
Adding more capabilities across the stack to differentiate from competitors and be a disruptor in the future.

Attaining Scale: Gain customer and market momentum at scale, displacing competitors, and future-proofing the acquirer for the near term while creating the runway for more game-changing acquisitions

Impact on M&A Integration

Ironically, the changing rules of business have not changed the mindset during integration a lot. It is still hovering around two schools of thought i.e., leave the target alone or absorb it at the speed of light running the playbook from 2017 which does not scale to create value in 2023!

In my experience, the M&A integration process must undergo these shifts to adapt towards value creation:

Integration Strategy

Scope M&A integrations are defined when specific products, customers, channels, and brands are added which differ from the current model, scale integrations are when similar products, customers, etc. are added to attain scale. Arguably all disruptive technology integrations are scope categories, but the integration degree may vary by situations outlined below.

Level of Integration	Situation
No integration	No experience with acquiring disruptive technologies; The first deal to catalyze the transition to a new business model
Limited integration	Scope integration rather than the scale integration i.e., investing where both companies benefit from the synergies
Partial integration	enhancing existing value chain in very specific areas, functions, processes, or value drivers; Be more surgical
Full integration	Experience with integration of multiple disruptive technologies; Major disruption to the existing business model while 'stimulating new capabilities

Figure 14: Integration Levels

Synergies

Traditionally companies have thought of synergies as cost or revenue only and approached it that way. Given there are typically no cost synergies (probably negative synergies due to underinvestment in back-office etc.) when acquiring smaller disruptive companies/technologies/business models, one needs to think about this differently. An approach I have frequently used is to look at synergies in three ways.

- Sequential synergies: If the acquirer (or target) does activity A, then the target (or acquirer) is now enabled to do activity B (sequential to A) previously impossible on the value chain.
- Reciprocal synergies: Acquirer brings X enabling Y for target and vice versa i.e., what can they both add to each other.

With this framework cost and revenue synergies are a byproduct, not a starting point, unlike traditional M&A integrations.

One other place to pay attention to is BETA synergies i.e., the collection of those reciprocal and sequential synergies that directly affect the equity profile or stock price. Isolate these value drivers upfront and track/measure/monitor/report them with more rigor while building them into the investor messaging.

Integration Management Office

Given the dynamics with integration, synergies, etc. there is an obvious impact on the IMO design and configuration.

- Lack of conventional synergies lead to break down of the rigid functional configuration of the IMO, it is now all about having value driver being the workstreams as opposed to the functions. Gone are the days when six functional boxes were solid lined into an IMO!

- Many M&A professionals both in corporate, and professional services need to know separate value creation from just protecting value for Day One or focusing on the IMO process e.g., governance, reporting, tracking, playbook, checklists, etc. While the IMO can turn the cranks, provide structure, rigor, reporting, etc., and is still important It is the value driver work streams (and applicable functions) that create shareholder value when acquiring disruptive technologies or business models.

Leading Practices: From Experience and Industry Network

A lot of the transactions I have been part of and a few insights from my network in the Silicon Valley revealed five success factors when acquiring disruptive and business model-changing technologies. The entire M&A continuum needs to adapt to the new world order, some insights:

- Building in-house capabilities on the disruptive technologies and around targets in the acquisition pipeline
- Conduct rigorous Technology diligence and go across the stack and evaluate for scalability, stability, interoperability, security, extensibility, performance, etc.
- Proactively develop a range of new valuation models
- Develop proactive board, investor messaging and education during M&A strategy development; the initial set of transactions can be less accretive.

- Develop specific integration approaches, do not run the traditional playbook.

25

Cloud Computing Risk and Opportunities in M&A

Cloud computing has revolutionized the way business is conducted creating opportunities to scale without adding more depreciating hardware on their books. However, migrating to the cloud is often underestimated and misunderstood. Many old economy companies embark on cloud migrations for the wrong reasons including a quest to drive up valuations, these moves can backfire degrading valuations and creating negative synergies. Here are some of the well-known red flags to examine while evaluating M&A targets.

Cloud Strategy

The cloud strategy owned by IT is a challenge. In the digital era, businesses run on cloud computing, and if they do not own the strategy, operations, and outcome it can create unforeseen challenges. Typical examples include lifting and shifting legacy architectures not built to operate in the new environment resulting in small CAPEX transforming into gargantuan OPEX reflecting directly on the business P/L. This sort of cloud strategy results in revenue stalling, profitability erosion, and customer dissatisfaction. When you hear terms like Kubernetes becoming synonymous with Cloud strategy, it is typically a red flag.

Cost Strategy

If the cloud strategy is driven by cost containment alone, then most legacy applications must be retired and cloud-native SaaS applications must be commissioned from third-party vendors, this reflects direct benefits on application maintenance headcount and near elimination of routine, IT runs. Economies of scale from one to many can be leveraged with immaculate ease spreading costs of running a single legacy application over hundreds of enterprises- grade applications. SaaS providers use the inverse of this principle spreading their operational costs over thousands of customers. Should a fit-for-purpose application not be available in the market, serverless computing must be deployed for efficiency, uptime, and speed. If a company has multiple on-premises applications, legacy, and no serverless then opportunities to pivot to the leaner posture must be examined. For acquirers and investors, there is substantial alpha in this pivot.

Revenue Strategy

Cloud computing strategy for revenue growth is one of the core principles in the digital era. The problems addressed by a technology stack within one company can also tap into the ecosystem of partners, vendors, suppliers via APIs to solve problems across single or multiple industries. The digital revenue engine requires ecosystem thinking with a broader vision. If the cloud strategy of the company is driven by revenue, then the monetization of digital revenue and ecosystem design must be examined. The absence of APIs and integrations are evident red flags pointing to a lack of vision, skills, or ability to execute and will affect revenue synergies after the M&A transaction is consummated.

Headcount Strategy

In the old economy, traditional IT departments kept the lights on and built technology in-house to protect or create a competitive advantage. The skills running mail servers, networks, legacy applications, and old data center operations are less relevant in the digital era, automation and SaaS applications have taken over the mundane. Legacy executives armed with the old-economy thought process continues to run large headcount-driven organizations. These heads are justified in the name of Kubernetes, migrations, and issues with SaaS vendors, etc. If the cloud strategy was about headcount reduction, becoming asset-lean then one must delve deeper into the heavy headcount posture of the company, Kubernetes cannot justify a cloud headcount strategy becoming an IT employment strategy. One must also examine headcount from vendors and creep within shadow IT organizations.

Security Strategy

One of the most widely debated topics in the industry is cloud security. Many organizations have moved to the cloud but leverage traditional security approaches which rarely factor in unique challenges with the cloud. As the cloud enables developers the freedom, speed, and agility to innovate it changes the security considerations from the past which addressed data centers, virtual perimeters, and controls leaning on equipment on-premises. Security skills and talent in many old-economy companies are not geared to understand risks stemming from provisioning, a multitude of security configurations across CI/CD pipelines, automation, third-party integrations, and a whole bunch of agile policies required for the modern era. Analyzing the skills of the individuals within the security organization is usually telling on where the target organization's maturity to deal with cloud security issues may be.

Deployment Strategy

The architecture and deployment of a truly multi-tenant model have significant benefits. However, many digital companies have their deployment botched. While this is situation is prevalent in older and mature start-ups who have multiple cloud instances built out for multiple customers with custom versions of each, many legacy players are also guilty of these issues. A SaaS wrapper on a piece of software can masquerade as a subscription model, but not true multi-tenant and scalable SaaS as it simply will not scale. Watch out for these issues when the M&A target seeks those premium SaaS valuation multiples.

Metrics to Watch

As you continue with the due diligence of the company's cloud posture, one must understand which cloud strategy was the primary driver. The four broad areas of metrics to examine are revenue, cost, assets, and headcount with specific KPIs under each area mapped to risks and opportunities about the cloud strategy its operations, health, and potential impact on the post-transaction mechanics for value creation.

Concluding Thoughts

The digital era has unleashed many companies which scale rapidly through adopting cloud computing for speed, scale, and efficiency. Implementing a sound cloud computing strategy and execution can create a winner that takes all, a poor cloud strategy can create high costs and post-M&A misery. One must stress test a target's cloud strategy through all lenses during the M&A due diligence.

26

M&A Deal Leakage

Introduction

M&A executives and professionals have always been trained about protecting the integrity of Deal information and leaking any information about a transaction cross that ethical red line. However, data and facts portray a different picture. Running the right process, having the right security controls, and having well-trained teams with a clean conscience can ensure no leakage in M&A information.

M&A Deal leaks are more common than one might expect even after regulatory oversight and laws governing insider trading. According to a 2020 report from Intralinks, approximately 8-10% of Deal information leaks globally and this has followed the last 8 years. Europe and Asia have fared far worse than the United States over years.

Types of Leakage

There are multiple reasons for M&A Deal leakage, despite the best efforts and intentions of Deal teams, bankers, attorneys, advisors, and consultants, etc. There are two broad categories intentional leaks and accidental leaks.

Intentional leaks are propagated out by insiders with intricate knowledge of the deal, intentions can vary from transaction sabotage, alerting rivals, etc. Accidental leaks are not driven by clear motivations, but carelessness around information protection systems and humans. From my observations, Deals leak mostly in their later stages i.e., after term-sheet rather than the upfront acquisition intent stage. There are also visible symptoms before the public announcement e.g. increased surge in trading volume of target company shares targeting bid premiums as the alpha. A classic example of an accidental deal leak was Salesforce's entire target scan deck being published on the internet via human and systemic deficiencies.

Wider access to corporate email calendars, meeting room calendars, social media posts with location tags all raise rumors, suspicions, and leaks. Once there is a rumor, validation becomes easier. None of these may break a deal, but open speculations, accusations, and room for sabotage too.

M&A Leakage Drivers

While accidental leakage is truly accidental, the intentional leakage has well thought out motives and drivers around them. The intentional leaks are originated from insiders who also know the risks and consequences. Let us examine a select few of these motives and drivers.

Valuation Premiums
Data also validates that leaked deals secured higher acquisition premiums over the non-leaked M&A transactions. According to the Intralinks report, median premiums on leaked deals was 48.2% while non-leaked deals commanded only 23.5%. These ranges in differential have been consistent across several years. An acquisition premium gap as substantial as this does motivate behavior changes across stakeholders.

More Bidders
This is the obvious and most effective reason behind deal leakage, more competitive bids lay the foundation for premiums. Intentional leaks raise the probability for rival bids, as rumors propagate more bidders join the race pushing acquisition prices higher. A good enough motivation for multiple constituents to deliver.

Executives and Management

Deal leaks are considered market abuse and could expose executives and the company to legal risk and financial consequences. Investor confidence and market image could come under scrutiny and most executives understand this. However, if you can examine the track records of management and executives from one deal leak and follow their career across multiple companies, the patterns of leakage have remarkable consistency!

Time to Close

While the odds of completing closure may not drastically vary, leaks do pressure the timelines to close. This aspect specifically becomes interesting when multiple tax situations of entities, executives, and transaction personnel are analyzed and understood depending on the time of the year and dates the closure is expected to march towards. Sellers want to expedite the Deal and close at the highest price.

Risks and Impact

Market abuse can have serious ramifications if done with nefarious motives e.g., drive up valuation, alter competitive dynamics, etc. M&A insiders have been fined by regulators on multiple occasions for leaking information, executives have been fired and there is an absolute wider consensus that intentional leaks might not be worth the stigma and reputational risk.

Once media has processed the leaks, the announcement day reduces enthusiasm from them, and analysts and stock prices get baked in with a limited uptick.

Managing M&A leaks commence by setting the tone at the top, right from the CEO. The NDA language, penalty clauses, advisor fee impact, and lower purchase price clauses can all be woven into transaction engagement terms as deterrents. Use ongoing communication and a robust set of systems and tools to manage access control to the flow of information during M&A.

Concluding Thoughts

The overall lure of leaking M&A deals continues to be lucrative, across many years data and observations have revealed that leaks are on the rise. Increased regulations, reputation risk, and enforcement have not proved to deter the situation completely and at least not with global consistency. Risks far outweigh benefits, especially larger deals in public markets. M&A leaks also trigger rival bids and enhanced valuations with takeover premiums paid by rivals and based on these factors, M&A deal leaks are expected to rise as years progress and will likely take an enhanced enforcement framework to mitigate.

NITIN KUMAR

27

M&A Competitive Anchors

Introduction

The M&A world is changing, yet integration is executed the old way with a dated playbook focusing on cost synergies and functional approaches with limited attention paid to shareholder value. Given that most old economy companies now aspire to undertake digital transformation, acquisitions are one of the preferred routes to acquiring new capabilities. These new M&A transactions require a core competitive anchor which can be tied to value drivers and finally to shareholder value. The anchor enforces value drivers to align with shareholder value even when synergies are not present in the conventional way e.g., high-valuation technology M&A deals with little back office costs and headcount.

Defining Competitive Anchors in M&A

Competitive anchors distinctly convey the new identity and brand promise to the market and investors clearly e.g., survive, maintain, and grow, etc. Competitive anchors help answer the question "what allows the NewCo. To consistently beat the competition?" i.e., how does the transaction provide a right to win? They are sufficiently detailed to outline unique sources and sustainable competitive advantages and shareholder value delivery potential.

They are a strategic tool applied to the overall business (not at a function or regional level), any M&A transaction can have more than one anchor and they are not exclusionary.

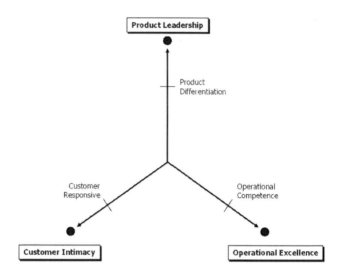

The Competitive Anchor Framework

Types of Competitive Anchors

There are multiple competitive anchors, each M&A transaction may have more than one. If a company is acquiring several targets as a part of its digital transformation journey, one must leave room and factor in anchors from subsequent acquisitions. Let us examine a non-exhaustive, but common list of competitive anchors.

Operational Excellence (best total cost)

Companies that focus on reliable, middle-of-the-market products at competitive prices delivered with minimal difficulty or inconvenience offer a low price and hassle-free service proposition. These companies focus on core processes such as product supply, expedient customer service, and demand management to provide their customers with the best experience. Examples of companies that have succeeded in this space include Fed Ex, Walmart, and McDonald's, all of whom have built their businesses around making it easy and affordable for customers to get the products and services they need. By offering a combination of high-quality products, efficient customer service, and low prices, these companies have proved themselves to be industry leaders and continue to thrive in a competitive market.

Product Leadership (best product)

For companies always looking to push the boundaries of what is possible, the focus is on continually innovating and delivering the best product, period. This proposition is based on offering products either unknown, untried, or highly desirable to consumers. Such companies put significant effort into their core processes, including invention, product development, and market exploitation. Examples of companies that have mastered this approach include Intel, Nike, 3M, Sony, Motorola, and Johnson & Johnson. These companies have become synonymous with cutting-edge products and continue to push the limits of what is possible. By consistently introducing new and innovative products year after year, they have set themselves apart in a highly competitive market and continue to be leaders in their respective industries.

Customer Intimacy (best customer experience)

Companies that focus on products specifically tailored to individual customers, rather than following what the broader market wants, focus on cultivating long-term relationships with their clients. These companies specialize in satisfying unique needs that only they - through their close relationship with the customer - recognize and build loyalty. The proposition they offer is not just the best solution, but also includes all the support needed to get the ideal value and results from the product. Core processes for these companies include personalized services and relationship management, which are critical to their success. Examples of companies that have excelled in this approach include Nordstrom, Airborn Express, Home Depot, and Cable & Wireless. These companies understand that personalized service and relationship building is essential to creating customer loyalty, and they focus on providing the best experience for their clients. By doing so, they have built strong and long-lasting relationships that have helped them stand out in their respective industries.

	Operational Excellence	Product Leadership	Customer Intimacy
Value Proposition	Best total cost	Best product	Best customer experience
Golden Rule	Variability kills efficiency	Cannibalize your own success with breakthrough revenue models	Solve problems beyond core issues
Core Processes	End-to-end product delivery Customer service cycle	Invention Commercialization Market exploitation	Customer acquisition, retention, and growth CX solution development
Improvement Levers	Process redesign Continuous improvement	Product innovation R&D cycle time	Problem expertise Personalized service

Examples of Competitive Anchors

Critical Success Factors

When competitive anchors are applied to M&A integration, the operating model must be less rigid as it must leave room to accommodate new competitive anchors and value drivers from subsequent acquisitions. Let us examine some of the core attributes and critical success criteria around the competitive anchor approach.

- The M&A integration planning must hinge on the competitive anchors as shareholder value and sustained competitive advantage will be resultant of the execution
- Focus on the core process of digital innovation, invention, product development, and market exploitation is a must.
- Loosely configured business structure (not a rigid org design rooted in older hierarchical principles) to accommodate ever-changing internal and external shifts. This will also allow entrepreneurial initiatives and redirections that characterize unexplored territory.
- Management systems that are results-driven to measure and reward product success and that don't punish the experimentation required to deliver.
- A culture that encourages individual imagination, accomplishment, out-of-

the-box thinking, and a mindset driven by the desire to create the future.

Leading Practices

Once the M&A integration process is nearing completion one must weave the anchors into the operating model of the sponsoring business with measurable and tactical actions. For example,

- Continually strive to provide its market with leading-edge products or useful new applications of existing products or services
- Creative, recognizing, and embracing ideas wherever they originate (inside or outside the company)
- Commercialize ideas quickly (supported by business and management processes geared for speed)
- Relentlessly pursue ways to leapfrog their own latest product or service (prefer to render their own products

obsolete than must have someone else do it)

- Measure success along with M&A integration teams every quarter to determine the quality and fit of the competitive anchors

Concluding Thoughts

Competitive anchors are the new structural elements from which value drivers are spawned, the advantage of setting the anchors also set shareholder value as the north star. Historically many M&A leaders have taken the value driver approach which has driven synergies. However, in many new deals, there are no conventional synergies but deal valuations are high with shareholders expecting returns, the competitive anchor approach makes sense as a discipline as M&A evolves and deal signatures depart from the conventional economic logic.

Can I Ask a Favor?

If you enjoyed this book, found it useful, or otherwise then we would appreciate it if you would post a short review on Amazon.

I do read all the reviews personally so we can continually write what people are wanting.

Thanks for your support!

About the Author

Nitin Kumar is a two-decade veteran in the Hi-Tech industry, he serves on boards and is a well-established CEO having led multiple global companies.

In his prior career as a Management Consulting Partner, he served many Corporate and Private Equity clients. Nitin has added value to over 1000 M&A deals spanning Consolidation Plays, Adjacency Moves, Technology Tuck-ins, New Business Model Transition, Distressed M&A, Acqui-hires, Hostile Takeovers, and Activist Offense/Defense. He has also led high-profile and complex divestitures.

He has won several international awards for pioneering new approaches in the M&A discipline and is considered one of the global thought leaders in this discipline.

Nitin is a Certified M&A Advisor, a Chartered M&A Professional, a Certified Post Merger Integration Professional, a Certified M&A Specialist, and a Certified Due Diligence Professional.

Thank You

Made in the USA
Columbia, SC
08 September 2024

42005561R00137